PERSONAL APPLI

THE BOOK OF GENESIS

COMPREHENSIVE WORKBOOK

DR. CHUCK MISSLER

The Book of Genesis

Comprehensive Workbook

© 2004 Koinonia House
P.O. Box D, Coeur d'Alene, Idaho 83816-0347   1-800-546-8731

How to Use this Workbook

For maximum benefit, please read the following tips:

1. Before starting a Genesis session, please read through the study questions and, if part of a small group, the discussion questions that pertain to that session.

2. The first section of each session is designed to help you take notes. You will discover that there is much more information than space provided, so it may be helpful to have extra paper on which to write.

3. If you are a small group leader, please feel free to use the questions at the back of the workbook to facilitate discussion within your group. See the *Discussion Questions for Small Group Leaders* section.

4. Through arrangements with Louisiana Baptist University, we can now offer you the means to earn college course credit toward a degree up to and including the Ph.D. through our Koinonia Institute. If you are interested in obtaining college credit for this study course(s), you will need to follow these steps:

    a) Email registrar@khouse.org to receive an application packet, which includes applications to both KI and LBU (.pdf files), the link to LBU's online catalog (www.lbu.edu), plus a list of available courses through Koinonia Institute.

    b) Fill out both applications and return to us with your $100 registration fee, which enrolls you in both KI and LBU. Tuition is $75 per credit. LBU will accept all KI course transcripts and is the institution that will grant your degree (you will still need to take distance-learning classes through LBU to earn your degree).

    c) This Genesis study is actually two college courses: BIB 201: Genesis Chapters 1-11 (sessions 1-14) and BIB 202: Genesis Chapters 12-50 (sessions 15-24). Each course is 3 credits = $225 in tuition per course, or $450 for both courses.

    d) After registration fee and tuition have been paid, finish all study questions in the main section of the workbook, as well as the additional assignments located in the *Koinonia Institute* section. These materials will be turned in, graded, and returned to the student along with a final exam. Once the final has been returned and graded, you will be notified of your grade in the course. For more information on procedures, see the information page at the front of the *Koinonia Institute* section of this workbook.

Only 2 World Views

- Everything is a result of a cosmic accident

- We are the result of a deliberate design by a Designer

The Central Theme

- The OT is an account of a Nation.
- The NT is the account of a Man.
- The Creator became a Man. His appearance is the Central Event of all history.
- He died to purchase us and is alive now.
- The most exalted privilege is to know Him. That's what the Bible is all about.

"Equidistant Letter Sequence?"

```
Rips explained that each
code is a case of adding
every fourth letter to
form a word.

     Read the code
```

Documentary Hypothesis
(Graf-Wellhausen Hypothesis)

- Compiled by later editors?
  - J   Jehovahist, Yahwist
  - E   Elohist
  - D   Deuteronomic source
  - P   Priestly source
  - J1, J2, E1, E2, P1, P2, K, L, N, S...
- Without any compelling historical, linguistic or textual evidence
- Shredded by Oswalt T. Allis; R. N. Whybray; E.J. Young, Umbertos Cassuto, RK Harrison, Kenneth A Kitchen… et al.

Textual Rebuttals

- Emmaus Road
- Authentication of Moses:
  - Mt 8:4; 19:7,8; 23:2; Mk 1:44; 10:3,4; 7:10; Lk 5:14; 16:19, 31; 20:37; 24:27,44; Jn 3:14; 5:39,45,46; 6:32; 7:19, 22,23.
- All Scriptures are Christ Centered:
  - Jn 5:39; Ps 40:7; Mt 5:17,18.
- OT Quotes:
  - Adam: Deut, Job, 1 Chr.
  - Noah: 1 Chr, Isa, Ezek.
  - Abraham: 15X in OT; 11X in NT.
  - Jacob: 20X in OT; 17X NT.
- NT Quotes of Genesis:
  - 165 direct quotes; ~200 allusions;
  - ~100 of the first 11 chapters.

New Testament References

- **The Creator and the Creation**
  - Matt 13:35; Mark 13:19; John 1:3; Acts 4:24; Acts 14:15; Rom 1:20; 2 Cor 4:6; Col 1:16; Heb 1:10; 11:3;
- **Allusions to the Creation**
  - Rom 1:25; 16:25; Eph 3:9; 1 Tim 4:4; Heb 2:10; 4:10; 9:26; James 3:9; Rev 3:14; 4:11; 10:6; 14:7
- **Creation of Man and Woman**
  - Matt 19:4-6, 8; Mark 10:6; Acts 17:26; 1 Cor 6:16; 11:8,9; Eph 5:31; 1 Tim 2:13, 14; Rev 2:7; 22:2, 14
- **The Fall**
  - Rom 5:11, 14, 17, 19; 8:19-20; 1 Cor 15:21-22; 2 Cor 11:3; Rev 20:2
- **The Flood**
  - Matt 24:37; Luke 17:26; 1 Pet 3:20; 2 Pet 2:5; 3:5-6
- **The Patriarchs**
  - Matt 23:35; Luke 3:34-38; 11:52; Heb 11:4-7, 23; 12:24; 1 John 3:12; Jude 11, 14

Genesis Session 1

Why Genesis?
The Book of Beginnings

Genesis vs. Revelation

	Gen	Rev
• Earth Created	1:1	
• Earth Passed away		21:1
• Sun to govern Day	1:16	
• No need of sun		21:23
• Darkness called night	1:5	
• No night there		22:5
• Waters He called seas	1:10	
• No more sea		21:1
• A river for earth's blessing	2:10-14	
• A river for New Earth		22:1,2

The Panorama of History

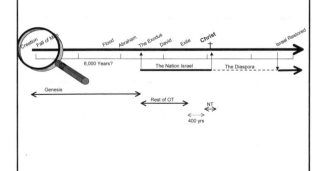

The Nature of Reality

A Glimpse of Hyperspaces

Time is *not* uniform

- Time is a *physical* property
- Time *varies* with
  - Mass
  - Acceleration
  - Gravity
    …among other things…
- We exist in *more* than 3 dimensions
  - Apparently, 10…

The Geometry of Eternity

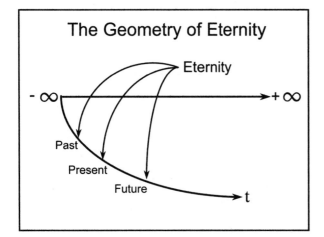

Genesis 1:1

> In the beginning God created the heaven and the earth.
>
> בְּרֵאשִׁית בָּרָא אֱלֹהִים אֵת הַשָּׁמַיִם וְאֵת הָאָרֶץ׃
>
> Genesis 1:1

- בְּרֵאשִׁית *Beresheet* = In beginning…
- בָּרָא *Bara* = Create out of nothing
  vs.
  Asa = make, fashion, fabricate of
  Yatsa = form (Isa 43:7 has all three)
- אֱלֹהִים *Elohim* = Plural noun, used as a singular

The Stretch Factor
(re: Dr. Gerald Schroeder)

- The expansion factor: ~10^{12}
- 16 billion years x 365 = 6,000,000,000,000 days
- 6 x 10^{12} days ÷ 10^{12} = 6 days

Exponential Expansion:
$$T = \int_0^t T_0 \, e^t$$

Day One	8 billion years
2nd Day	4 billion years
3rd Day	2 billion years
4th Day	1 billion years
5th Day	½ billion years
6th Day	¼ billion years
	15 ¾ billion years

Young Earth Indicators
- Moon Dust
- Oil Gushers
- Earth's Magnetic Field
- Mississippi River Delta
- Salinity of Oceans
- Poynting-Robertson Effect
- Radiohalos

Velocity of *c* Decreasing

- Four of five related atomic properties dependent upon c have demonstrated decrease;
- Slowing of atomic clocks relative to orbital clocks
  - If atomic clocks are correct, orbital speeds of Mercury, Venus and Mars are increasing
- Quantization of Red Shift
- Distortion of gravity during an early expansion phase
  - Time stands still at event horizon

The "Molten Sea"
1 Kings 7:23

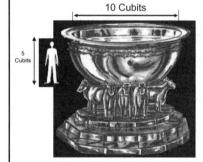

10 Cubits
5 Cubits

Circumference =
3 x diameter? No!
π x diameter
π = 3.14159265358979

e (mathematics)

The number *e* is most commonly defined as the limit of the expression

$(1 + 1/n)^n$

as *n* becomes large without bound.

This limiting value is approximately 2.7182818285

The number *e* forms the base of natural, or Napierian, logarithms.

Genesis Session 1

The Book of Genesis: Introduction

1) What are the (only) two world views? What four questions inevitably derive from them?

2) What two discoveries of the Bible underpin these studies?

3) Who wrote the Torah? How do we know for sure?

4) How do we know that time is a *physical* property? How does that impact our Biblical views?

5) Why do most people believe in a very "old" universe? (List the primary reasons.)

6) What does thermodynamics indicate about the age of the universe?

7) List at least five indicators that suggest a "young" earth.

Group Discussion Questions: See *Small Group Leaders* section of this workbook.

Preparation for the Next Session:

Read Genesis 1; Isaiah 14, 45; Ezekiel 28; and, Jeremiah 4. Review any available background on the nature of light.

Genesis Session 2

Session 2:

Genesis
Day One
Chapter 1:2-5

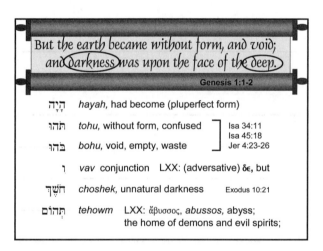

Some Basic Issues
- When were the angels created?
- When did Satan Fall?
- Is there a "gap" between v.1 and v.2?

Satan

His Origin, Agenda, and Destiny

And the earth was without form, and void; and darkness was upon the face of the deep.

And the Spirit of God moved upon the face of the waters.

And God said, Let there be light: and there was light.

Genesis 1:2,3

מְרַחֶפֶת *Merahefet*: to hover above, flutter, brood, vibrate

---

Two-Slit Experiment

20th Century Reversal

- 1900: Max Planck's desperate misapplication of Boltzmann's equations worked (revealing non-continuity)
- Albert Einstein publishes on Planck in 1904: leads to a revival of the corpuscular theory of light.
  - Energy is not continuous: only in *quanta*
  - Opens the door to the paradoxical world of "Quantum Physics."

Velocity of Light?

- 17th century: Johannes Kepler, Rene Descartes, et al, believed light was instantaneous ("c" was infinite).
- 1677: Olaf Roemer measured elapsed time between eclipses of Jupiter with its moons, yielding a *finite* speed of light.
- 1729: James Bradley confirmed Roemer's work.
- Over 300 years, measured 164 times by 16 different methods.

Setterfield-Norman Analysis

- 1677, Roemer, Io eclipse:
  − 307,600 +/- 5400 km/sec
- 1875, Harvard, (same method):
  − 299,921 +/- 13 km/sec
- 1983, National Bureau of Standards, laser:
  − 299,792.4586 +/- 0.00003 km/sec

Atomic vs Orbital Time

- Until 1967 (Orbital time):
  1 sec = 1/31,556,925.9747 of one earth orbit around the sun
- After 1967 (Atomic time):
  1 sec = 9,192,631,770 oscillations of the cesium-133 atom

- If atomic clocks are "correct": the orbital speeds of Mercury, Venus, and Mars are *increasing*.
- If the gravitational constant is truly constant, then atomic vibrations and the speed of light are *decreasing*.

Analogous Attributes

God	Light
Located at Infinity	No Parallax
Infinite Power	Velocity limit
Omnipresence	Photons lack locality
Omniscience	Fundamental Revelatory Mechanism

An Addendum:

Holography

A Provocative Analogy

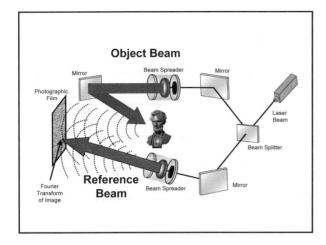

Communications Engineering

- The Bible as a Hologram
  - Fourier Transform Properties
  - Transcendent of Parallax
- Spread-spectrum Design
  - Exploitation of entire bandwidth
  - Immunity to hostile jamming

Information Measures

Entropy	Information
Disorder	Order
Noise	Signal
Cacophony	Music
Chaos	Cosmos
Randomness	Design

עֶרֶב *Erev*

- Obscuration, mixture; (increasing entropy); When encroaching darkness began to deny the ability to discern forms, shapes, and identities; hence:
- Twilight; the time of approaching darkness Prov 7:9; Jer 6:4
- Sunset; marking the duration of impurity: when a ceremonially unclean person became clean again Lev 15
- The beginning of the Hebrew day

בֹּקֶר *Boker*

- Becoming discernable, distinguishable, visible; perception of order; relief of obscurity; (decreasing entropy); attendant ability to begin to discern forms, shapes, and distinct identities; breaking forth of light; revealing; hence:
- Dawn; morning Gen 19:27; Kgs 19:9

Entropy Profile of the Universe

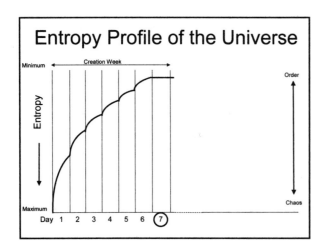

Genesis Session 2: Day One

Genesis 1:2-5

1) Why do some believe that there may have been a "gap" between Genesis 1:1 and 1:2?

2) What are the arguments against it?

3) What do we know about the origin of Satan? How do we know?

4) How many angels fell with Satan in his rebellion? How do we know?

5) What makes the nature of light paradoxical?

6) What are the reasons light is viewed as a stream of particles? What are the reasons that light behaves as a wave phenomena?

7) What are the implications if, indeed, the velocity of light has been decreasing through the ages?

8) Give examples of the entropy laws in everyday life.

9) Contrast the terms "erev" and "boker" as they are used in Genesis One. Why are they *unlikely* to simply signify "evening" and "morning"?

Group Discussion Questions: See *Small Group Leaders* section of this workbook.

Preparation for the Next Session:

Review Genesis 1. Review any available introductory literature on the nature of space and/or quantum physics.

Session 3:

Genesis
2nd Day
Chapter 1:6-8

Alternative "Days"

Ages Hypothesis
- Days 1-3: no sun
- 7th day: no "evening and morning"
- Framework Hypothesis
  - Disjunction between "literal" and "literary"
    - Parallelism: initial 3 & last 3
    - No rain, no plants, etc.   Gen 2:5
  - Scenario to an Earth-observer
- Literal 24-hours   Ex 20:11

מַיִם *mayim*

- Meaning:
  - water, waters
  - danger, violence, transitory things
- Origin: dual of a primitive noun (a plural form always used in a singular sense)
- Metaphor or synecdoche?
  - Vocabulary for plasma?
    - 4th state of matter: pre-molecules, etc.

Thermal Profile of Water

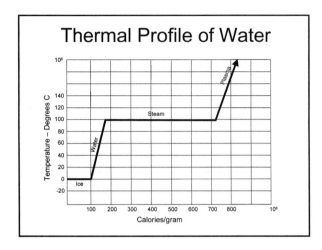

Model of the Atom

(Not to scale!)

Atom: 10^{-8}
Nucleus: $\dfrac{10^{-13}}{10^{-5}}$

Volume: $(10^5)^3 = 10^{15}$

Symmetry of Design

- Each particle has an antiparticle:

  particle + antiparticle $\xleftrightarrow{?}$ annihilation + photon

- Reversibility could imply that light could have created them "out of nothing."

Non-locality

- 1964: John Stewart Bell, CERN, Geneva, formulated a mathematical approach to demonstrating non-locality: "The Bell Inequality"
- 1982: Alain Aspect, Jean Dalibard, and Gérard Roger at the Institute of Theoretical and Applied Optics, Paris, conducted a landmark experiment:
  - **The Two-Particle Experiment**
    - Twin photons from heating cesium atoms with lasers, each traveled in opposite directions through 6.5 meters of pipe to special polarization analyzers.
    - Filters switched in 10 nanoseconds, 30 nanoseconds *less* than the 13 meters of travel between them.
- Photons *did* demonstrate non-locality.

Separation:
רָקִיעַ *raqia* & מַיִם *mayim*

- Canopy theory
  - Waters above the earth
  - Heaven = atmospheric sense
    - Atmosphere;
    - Sky; region of stars, etc
    - Heaven; Throne of God
- Fabric of Space itself

The Fabric of Space

A History of
The Aether Hypotheses

The Nature of Light

- Light "particles" could traverse a pure vacuum without the necessity of a real medium pervading space.
- But other experiments soon began to show that light was a wave phenomenon.
  - at the time only compressional waves were imagined but light waves proved to be transverse.
- In parallel with all these growing controversies, the velocity of light was finally measured by Olaf Roemer in 1675 and found to be finite
  - although the values he obtained were a few percent higher than the present value of 299,792.4358 km/sec.

"Zero-Point" Energy

- If the temperature of an empty container is lowered to absolute zero, there still remains a residual amount of thermal energy that can not by any means be removed: the "zero-point energy."
  - A "vacuum" is now known to be a vast reservoir of seething energy out of which particles are being formed and annihilated constantly.

Why doesn't the electron in an atom simply radiate its energy away and spiral into the nucleus?

It picks up energy from the background zero-point energy and therefore is sustained by it.

"Stretching the Heavens"

- 2 Sam 22:10
- Job 9:8
- Job 26:7
- Job 37:18
- Psalm 18:9
- Psalm 104:2
- Psalm 144:5
- Isaiah 40:22
- Isaiah 42:5
- Isaiah 44:24
- Isaiah 45:12
- Isaiah 48:13
- Isaiah 51:13
- Jeremiah 10:12
- Jeremiah 51:15
- Ezekiel 1:22
- Zechariah 12:1

Hyperdimensions

Mr. & Mrs. Flat

How would you communicate a 3-dimensional Object to a 2-dimensional universe?

By a 2-dimensional projection?

Here is a 3-dimensional projection of a 4-dimensional hypercube.

Not very useful, is it?

Two Imputed Concepts
(Elusive in Our Physical World)

1. Randomness   Prov 16:33
   - Stochastic vs. Deterministic Processes
   - Pseudo-Random Numbers
   - "Chaos Theory"
2. Infinity   Jas 1:17
   - Macrocosm: Finite Universe
   - Microcosm: Quantum Physics

Planck length: 10^{-33} cm.
Planck time: 10^{-43} sec.

∴ *Digital* Simulation
   - "Reality" is only Virtual

The Holographic Universe

- David Bohm's Model
  - Explicate (Enfolded Order):
    - tangible everyday physical reality
  - Implicate (Unfolded) Order:
    - More primary, deeper, underlying reality
- Sympathetic Support:
  - Roger Penrose of Oxford
    - the creator of the modern theory of black holes;
  - Bernard d'Espagnat of the University of Paris
    - Leading authorities on foundations of quantum theory
  - Brian Josephson of University of Cambridge
    - Winner of the 1973 Nobel Prize in physics.

The "Big Bang" Models

"First there was nothing…

…And then it exploded…"

Risk Analysis

Actuality:	Conclusion: False	Conclusion: True
True	Type I Error	OK
False	OK	Type II Error

Type I Error: Rejecting a true hypothesis
Type II Error: Accepting a false hypothesis

J. Neyman and E. S. Pearson

Genesis Session 3: 2nd Day

Genesis 1:6-8

1) List the principal theories to explain the six "days" of Creation, and summarize the problems of each.

2) What are the principal arguments for literal days of the Creation?

3) What alternative meanings might "*mayim*" signify besides simply "water"?

4) What does "*raqia*" signify? What alternative meanings might it include?

5) What are the four primary states of matter? How do they differ?

6) List five basic physical properties of "empty" space.

7) What are "hyperspaces"? How do they impact our perspectives of Biblical topics?

8) What is meant by "non-locality" of particles? How do these discoveries impact our Biblical views?

9) Which two concepts in mathematics are elusive as far as our physical universe is concerned? How do they bound our understanding of reality?

Group Discussion Questions: See *Small Group Leaders* section of this workbook.

Preparation for the Next Session:

Read Genesis 1:9-13.

Genesis Session 4

The Beads of Waitangi

Impossibility of "Chance"

- Only 10^{18} seconds in the history of the universe
- Only 10^{66} atoms in our entire galaxy
- Only 10^{80} particles in our entire galaxy
- Probabilities $<10^{-50}$ defines "*absurd*"
- Specificity $\sim 10^{-650}$ far beyond "chance"
- = equal to winning the lottery *every day for 90 days in a row!*

The DNA Code

- 3-out-of-4 error-correcting self-replicating code
- Over 3 *billion* elements defining the manufacture and arrangement of hundreds of thousands of devices;
- Consisting of unique assemblies
  - selected from over 200 proteins;
  - each involving 3,000 atoms in 3-dimensional configurations,
  - all defined from an alphabet of 20 amino acids,

Laws of Thermodynamics

- 1st Law: Conservation
  Matter and Energy cannot be created or destroyed
  ("You can't win")
  Gen 2:2-3; Heb 4:3-4; Neh 9:6
- 2nd Law: Entropy
  All processes involve a loss
  ("You can't break even")
  Ps 103:25,26; Isa 51:6;
  Matt 24:35; Rom 8:21

A Jar of Peanut Butter

- An empirical test…

  Life ✘ Matter + Energy

  Life = Matter + Energy + *Information*

  The food industry conducts over a billion "experiments" each year, for over a century, relying on the fact that evolution is not just unlikely, but *impossible*.

Entropy Profile of the Universe

עֶרֶב *erev*, chaos, disorder (later, "evening")

בֹּקֶר *boker*, orderly, discernable (later, "morning")

Biblical Anticipations

- Water cycle — Ecc 1:6,7; Job 36:27, 28
- Jet Stream — Ecc 1:6-7
- Evaporation — Job 26:8, Eccl 1:6-7, Amo 9:6
- Source of River Water — Ecc 1:6-7
- Fresh-Water Springs in the Sea — Job 38:16
- Pathways in the sea — Psa 8:8; Isa 43:16

God's Science Quiz

- 77 questions in the final 4 chapters of Job
- Science's mandate: Gen 1:28
- Science, which should have been the great testimony to the majesty and glory of God, has, instead, become a device for ignoring and rejecting Him, and preying on the uninformed.

Allusions Included

Job 38:
- The rotation of the earth — 12-15
- The springs and pathways of the sea — 16
- The breadth of the earth — 18
- The travel of light — 19
- The dividing of light — 24
- The source of rain, and ice — 28-30
- The universal nature of physical laws — 33
- Electrical communications — 35

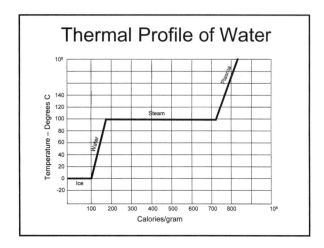

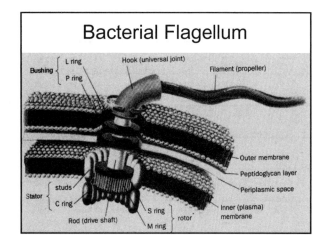

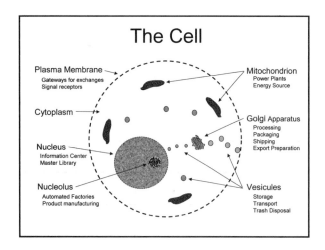

Tangle-free Handling?

- Equivalent to two strands of monofilament fishing line 125 miles long, stored inside a basketball;
- Unzipped, copied, and restored on spools (at 3 times the speed of an airplane propeller), *without tangling!*

Photosynthesis

- Means "To build with light":
  - Sugar factories producing millions of new glucose molecules/second
- Most plants produce more glucose than they use and store it as starch and other carbohydrates in roots, stems, and leaves.
- Each year photosynthesizing organisms produce about 170 billion metric tons of extra carbohydrates, about 30 metric tons for every person on earth.

2 Stage Process

- The Light-Dependent Reaction
  - A chloroplast traps light energy and converts it into chemical energy contained in two types of molecules
    - nicotinamide adenine dinucleotide phosphate (NADPH)
    - adenosine triphosphate (ATP)
- The Light-Independent Reaction
  - NADPH provides the hydrogen atoms that help form glucose,
  - ATP provides the energy for this and other reactions used to synthesize glucose

The Four Forces

- Gravity
- Electromagnetic
- Strong Nuclear Force
- Weak Nuclear Force

Green Bank Formula

$$N = R * f_p * n_e * f_l * f_c * L$$

N	Number of civilizations in our galaxy
R	Rate of star formation
f_p	fraction with planetary systems
n_e	mean planets with a life capable ecology
f_l	fraction on which life actually occurs
f_c	fraction on which intelligent beings develop to a communication phase
L	mean lifetime of technological civilizations

Trees in Genesis 2

אשל	Tamarisk (2)		רמון	Pomegranate (8)
אלה	Terebinth, (-2)		גפר	Gopherwood or fir (8)
עבת	Thicket (or Dense forest) (-3)		סנה	Thornbush [*Crataegus*] (9)
הדר	Citron (-3)		זית	Olive (-9)
שטה	Acacia (-3)		בטן	Pistachio Nut (13)
שקד	Almond (5)		לוז	Hazel (-13)
חטה	Wheat (5)		תאנה	Fig (14)
תמר	Date Palm(5)		ערבה	Willow (-15)
ארז	Cedar (-5)		אלון	Oak (17)
אהלים	Aloe (6)		גפן	Vine (-18)
ענב	Grape (-6)		שערה	Barley (-28)
אטד	Boxthorn or Bramble (7)		ערמו	Chestnut (44)
קדה	Cassia (7)		לבנה	Poplar (-85)

Genesis Session 4: 3rd Day

Genesis 1:9-13

1) What level of probability is defined by science as "absurd"?

2) Why is the hemoglobin molecule *less* likely to have occurred by unaided chance than the beads spelling, in Morse Code, Gen 1:1?

3) Why is the DNA molecule even *less* likely?

4) How does the 1st Law of Thermodynamics support the concept of Creation?

5) How does the 2nd Law of Thermodynamics refute a self-generating universe?

6) How does a jar of peanut butter disprove biogenesis?

7) Why does ice float? What would be the results if it didn't?

8) What *determines* the four states of matter?

9) What is the anthropic principle? How does it refute evolution by unaided chance?

Group Discussion Questions: See *Small Group Leaders* section of this workbook.

Preparation for the Next Session:

Review Genesis Chapter 1 again. Also, read Joshua 10 (the Long Day). Review a) the seven major Feasts of Moses and b) The Hebrew *Mazzeroth* (Zodiac).

Session 5:

Genesis

Fourth Day
Chapter 1:14-19

The Nebular Hypothesis

Difficulties Mount

- The sun contains 99.86% of all the mass of the solar system.
  - Yet the sun contains only 1.9% of the *angular momentum*.
  - The nine planets contain 98.1%.
  - (This was known in the time of Laplace a century ago.) There is no plausible explanation that would support a solar origin of the planets.
- James Jeans (1877-1946) pointed out that the outer planets are far larger than the inner ones.
  - Jupiter is 5,750 times as massive as mercury, 2,958 times as massive as Mars, etc.
  - This is also a difficulty with current theories.

Other Enigmas

- There are three *pairs* of rapid-spin rates among our planets, each within 3% of each other :
  - Earth and Mars,
  - Jupiter and Saturn, and
  - Neptune and Uranus. Why?
- Earth and Mars have virtually identical *spin axis tilts* (about 23.5°). Why?
- From angular momentum and orbital calculations, *it would seem that three pairs of these planets may have been brought here from elsewhere.*
- Why does Mars have 93% of its craters in *one hemisphere* and only 7% in the other?
  - It would appear that over 80% occurred *within a single half-hour!*

Uniformity Delusions

- View any surface in the solar system: craters and disruptive evidences
- Under a constant rain of interplanetary debris the Earth accumulates about 100 tons of extraterrestrial material per day.
- Over 100 craters on the Earth

The Long Day of Joshua

Mars Near Pass-Bys?

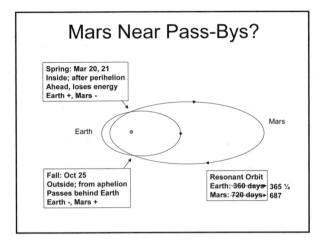

Spring: Mar 20, 21
Inside; after perihelion
Ahead, loses energy
Earth +, Mars −

Fall: Oct 25
Outside; from aphelion
Passes behind Earth
Earth −, Mars +

Resonant Orbit
Earth: ~~360 days~~ 365 ¼
Mars: ~~720 days~~ 687

Gulliver's Testimony

- Early Telescope Technology

1610	Galileo	4 Moons of Jupiter; Saturn's rings
1781	Hershel	Uranus
1787	"	2 Moons of Uranus
1789	"	2 more Moons of Uranus
1846	Laverrier	Neptune; 1 Moon
1877	Asaph Hall	2 Moons of Mars (Deimos & Phobos)
		Deimos: 30h18m (almost synchronous) orbit
		Phobos: 7h39m *eastward*; 8 mi dia.; 3% albedo

- Jonathan Swift (1667-1745)

  1726 *Gulliver's Travels, ("Voyage to Laputa")*:
  Details the size, revolutions, and orbits, of the 2 moons of Mars.
  151 years before they were discovered by astronomers!

The Long Day

- 1/3 of million men at Beth-Horon
- Oct 25, 1404 BC:
  – Mars on a polar pass at 70,000 miles
  – Appeared to rise *50 times* the size of Moon
  – Severe Earthquakes, land tides
  – Polar shift of 5°, "day" lengthened
  – Meteors follow 2-3 hrs later, @ 30,000 mph
- Included in other ancient legends and folklore
  – Long night of China

Spiral Galaxies

2 million light-years
18 million light-years
25 million light-years
32 million light-years
65 million light-years
106 million light-years

Galaxy Twist

- The furthest galaxies had to release their light long before the closer galaxies.
- The further galaxies did not have as much time to rotate and twist their arms.
- Thus, the closer galaxies should have the most twist.
- If the speed of light was a million times faster in the past, that would account for them being so similar...

The Mazzaroth

- All the stars have a name   Ps 147:4
                                Isa 40:26
- Zodiac: Ζωδιακος, from *Sodi*, "the Way"
- The Temple of Denderah, 2000 BC

Virgo, the Virgin

Alpha: *Spica* (ear of corn).
Hebrew: *Tsemech* (branch).
Arabic: *Al Zimach* (branch).
Egypt: *Aspolia* (the seed)

Of 20 Hebrew words translated branch, only *Tsemech* is used exclusively of the Messiah
Jer 23:5,6; Zech 3:8, 6:12; Isa 4:2

The Promised Seed of the Woman
Gen 3:15
with a *branch* in her right hand, ears of *corn* in her left.
John 12:21-24

The Message

- Virgo
  - The Seed of the Woman
  - The Desire of Nations
  - The Man of Double Nature in humiliation
  - The Exalted Shepherd and Harvester
- Libra
  - The Price to be paid
  - The Cross to be endured
  - The Victim slain
  - The Crown Purchased

הַמּוֹעֲדִים The Appointed Times

- Statistical expectation: 5 times in the 78,064 letters of Genesis;
- As an *equidistant letter sequence*, it appears **only once** in Genesis;
- At an interval of 70;
- It is centered on Genesis 1:14.
- Odds against this by unaided chance have been estimated at greater than *70,000,000 to one!*

The Feasts of Israel

The Spring Feasts   (1st Month: Nisan)
- Passover
- Feast of Unleavened Bread
- Feast of First Fruits

Feast of Weeks

The Fall Feasts   (7th Month: Tishri)
- Feast of Trumpets
- Yom Kippur
- Feast of Tabernacles

Months	Old	New	
Tishri, (Ethanim)	1	7	Sep-Oct
Cheshvan, (Bul)	2	8	Oct-Nov
Chisleu	3	9	Nov-Dec
Tevet	4	10	Dec-Jan
Sh'vat	5	11	Jan-Feb
Adar	6	12	Feb-Mar
Nisan, (Aviv)	**7**	**1**	Mar-Apr
Ilyar (Zif)	8	2	Apr-May
Sivan	9	3	May-Jun
Tammuz	10	4	Jun-Jul
Av	11	5	Jul-Aug
Elul	12	6	Aug-Sep

Israel: ישראל

- 1st 10,000 letters of Genesis, -100 to +100:
  - only twice: intervals of 7 and 50
  - *Kiddush*, The Sabbath observance
    Genesis 1:31 - 2:3
  - Jubilee Year, after 7 *Shmitas*
    Leviticus 25, 27

Genesis Session 5: 4th Day

Genesis 1:14-19

1) What is the "Nebular Hypothesis" and what are its major defects?

2) How does the "twist" of spiral galaxies suggest a "young" universe?

3) List the 70 "appointed times" on the Hebrew calendar. In what way were the Feasts of Israel *prophetic*?

4) What is the significance of the Ark of Noah coming to rest on the 17th day of the 7th month?

_____
_____
_____
_____
_____
_____
_____
_____

5) How could there have been a "long day" in Joshua's time while still maintaining the rotation of the earth?

_____
_____
_____
_____
_____
_____
_____
_____

6) What does Jonathan Swift's *Gulliver's Travels* have to do with our views of planetary motion?

_____
_____
_____
_____
_____
_____
_____
_____

Group Discussion Questions: See *Small Group Leaders* section of this workbook.

Preparation for the Next Session:

What are the major flaws in the theory of Evolution as an explanation of our origins? Prepare to discuss.

Session 6:

Genesis

Fifth Day
Chapter 1:20-23

Entropy Profile of the Universe

- Minimum / Maximum Entropy
- Creation Week — Day 1 2 3 4 5 6 7
- בֹּקֶר *boker*
- עֶרֶב *erev*
- Order / Chaos

A Watch versus the Wrist

Watch = simple open loop system

Wrist:
- Complex closed loop servo system
- Adapts to ambient conditions
- Fights off invaders
- Self-repairing

Evolutionary Fallacies

- Self-organization violates the Law of Entropy (2nd Law of Thermodynamics)

- Complex system assemblies *require all subsystems to be functional* for system survival.

Hierarchy of Design

- Open Loop Systems
- Closed Loop Systems
- Adaptive Systems
- Self-modifying Systems
- Intelligent Machines

Intelligent Machines

- Self-modifying Systems
- Self-programming Systems
- Self-diagnostic Systems
- Self-repairing Systems
- Self-reproducing Systems

Model of the Atom

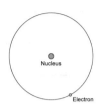

(Not to scale!)

Atom: 10^{-8}
Nucleus: $\dfrac{10^{-13}}{10^{-5}}$

Volume: $(10^5)^3 = 10^{15}$

The Destructive Villains

- Oxidation
- Ultraviolet Radiation
    - $3\ H_2O + UV \rightarrow 3\ H_2 + O_3$
- Water
- Reversibility
    - Amino Acid + Amino Acid $\leftrightarrow$ Protein + H_2O
    - Nucleotide + Nucleotide $\leftrightarrow$ DNA + H_2O
- Equilibrium: the enemy of selectivity
- Time

Molecular Chirality

Dextrorotary — All DNA/RNA Nucleotides
Levorotary — All amino acids in living proteins

The Cell Revealed

A Constellation of Miracles
in a Miniature City

Automated Factories in the Cell

- Robot Machines (hundreds of thousands of different types)
- Artificial languages and decoding systems
- Memory banks for information storage
- Elegant control systems regulating automated assembly of components
- Prefabrication and modular construction
- Error fail-safe and proof-reading devices for quality control

Digital Information Flow

"Crick Dogma"   Retrovirus

DNA   (master blueprint)
 | transcription
RNA   (photocopy)
 | translation
Proteins (functional machines)
  (Polypeptides of amino acid chains)

Tangle-free Handling?

- Equivalent to two strands of monofilament fishing line 125 miles long, stored inside a basketball;
- Unzipped, copied, and restored on spools (at 3 times the speed of an airplane propeller), *without tangling!*

Dinosaurs?

- Land-based
  - Behemoth   Job 40
- Sea-based
  - Leviathan   Job 41

New Zealand, 1977
  - 900 ft down
  - 32 ft long, 4,000 lbs

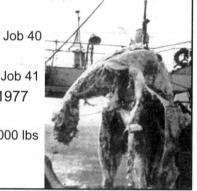

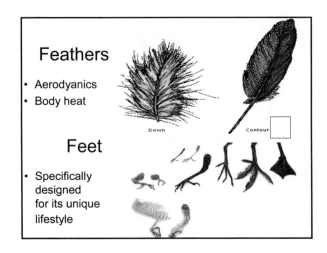

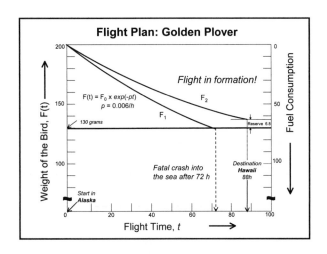

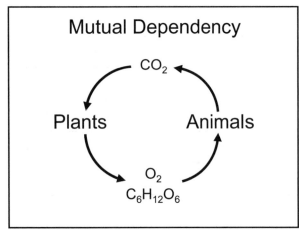

Genesis Session 6: 5th Day

Genesis 1:20 - 23

1) Contrast the views of Bishop William Paley and David Hume; which is more rational?

2) Explain the "levels of design" and why they argue against the role of unaided chance in complex systems.

3) What is the fallacy of "prebiotic soup" as the source of life?

4) What is "molecular chirality" and how does it refute randomness as a source of design?

5) How does a *digital* code refute randomness as a source of design?

Group Discussion Questions: See *Small Group Leaders* section of this workbook.

Preparation for the Next Session:

Re-read Genesis Chapter 1. Prepare to discuss the notion that man was the result of random, unaided chance processes.

Session 7:

Genesis

Sixth Day

Chapter 1:24-28

Animals

- Why, after 120 years of searching, no "missing links"?
  - *Digitally* defined
- Evidences of unique specific design *in each*...

Special Engineering

- Skull
- Teeth
- Horns
- Vertebrae
- Shoulder joint
- Forelegs
- "Wrist" bone

The Trinity

- Notice the plurals: "us"; "our"
  - Gen 1:26; 3:22; 11:7; Isa 6:8
  - Elohim (680 times)
- Singularity of OT? Deut 6:4-5; Ex 20:3
- Plurality of NT? Mt 28:19; 2 Cor 13:14; John 14-17, etc.
- Exchanges among the Godhead
  - Gen 3:22; 11:7; Isa 6:8; 48:12, 13, 16; Ps 2:7; 45:7; 110:1; Matt 11:27; John 8:42; John 17:24

Jesus Christ

- Made in the likeness of men
  - Phil 2:7; Heb 10:5; Luke 1:35
- Is the image of God
  - Heb 1:3; Col 1:15; 2 Cor 4:4
- Anticipated redemption
  - 1 Pet 1:20; Rev 17:8; 2 Tim 1:9

The Fibonacci Sequence

- 1180, Leonardo Fibonacci,
  - "Leonardo of Pisa"
- 1,1,2,3,5,8,13,21,34,55,89,144,233…
- Ratio of any adjacent numbers: ~1.618
  - $(1 + 5^{1/2})/2 = 1.618$
- *It would be several hundred years before these sequences would be recognized in nature*

Phyllotaxis

- Spiral arrangement of leaves around a plant's stem
  - Elm — ½ circumference
  - Beech, Hazel — 1/3
  - Apricot, Oak — 2/5
  - Pear, Poplar — 3/8
  - Almond, Pussy Willow — 5/13
  - Pines — 5/21 or 13/34
- 434 Angiospermae, 44 Gymnospermae:
  - all with Fibonacci numbers
- Maximizes exposure to sunlight and air without shading or crowding from other leaves

The Golden Spiral

- The Chambered Nautilus
- Hurricanes
- Spiral Seeds
- The Ram's horn
- Sea-horse tail
- Growing fern leaves
- DNA molecule
- Waves breaking on the beach
- Tornados
- Galaxies
- Tail of a comet around the sun
- Whirlpools
- Seed patterns of sunflowers, daisies, dandelions
- The ears of all mammals
- Cochlea of the human ear

System Dependencies

- Digestive System
- The Circulatory System
- The Respiratory System
- The Sensory Systems
  - Eyes, Ears, Proprioceptive System
- The Immune System
- The Nervous System

The Human Brain

- 10^{10} nerve cells
- *Each* with 10^4 - 10^5 connecting fibres
- Approaches 10^{15} connections

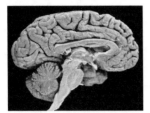

Further Conjectures

- Discerning internal vs. external realities?
- Imagination, inspiration, creativity go *beyond* storage, recall, and processing

[Conjecture: Hyperdimensional transfer function to other dimensions beyond our consciousness?]

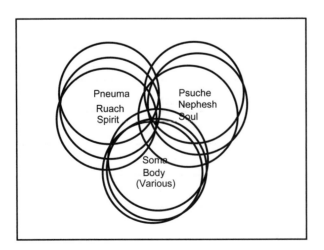

Genesis Session 7

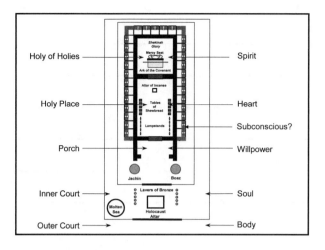

Computer Architecture

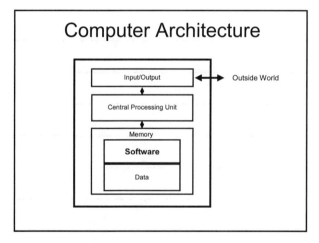

Software Characteristics

- Software includes self-modifying codes
- Software is generated from high level language layers into "machine code"
  - Its architecture cannot be inferred from its external behavior
- Software has no "mass"
  - It can be transmitted through the air waves

The Nature of Time

- Time is a *physical* dimension
- Time varies with
  - Mass
  - Acceleration
  - Gravity
- Software has *no* mass
  - It has no time dimension

The Physics of Immortality

- Frank J. Tipler, Professor of Mathematical Physics, Tulane University
  - Using the most advanced and sophisticated methods of modern physics, demands "in exactly the same way physicists calculate the properties of an electron" arrived at two conclusions about God and immortality:
    - 1) He discovered proof of the existence of God.
    - 2) *He also now believes that every human being who ever lived will be resurrected from the dead.*

Creation Completed

- "The 6th Day": Definite article used for the first time; stresses completion
- Onkelos Translation ("The Translation"): *"It was a unified order."*

Genesis Session 7: 6th Day

Genesis 1:24-28

1) Why is it unlikely that any Darwinian "missing links" will ever be found?

2) What peculiar design problems does a giraffe present, and how do they refute evolution as a source of design? Why couldn't these have been resolved by random processes?

3) What are the main references to the Trinity in the Bible? (Include those in the Old Testament.)

4) How is photosynthesis a refutation of evolution?

5) How is the co-dependency of plants and animals an evidence of skillful design?

6) How is the role of symmetry in nature a refutation of randomness as a source of "design"?

7) What are Fibonacci numbers and why are they significant? Give examples.

8) List the historical "monkey men" and the basis of regarding them as frauds.

9) List at least 8 complex interdependent systems of the human body and explain why they represent substantial design problems of their existence.

10) What are the three main architectural elements of (Mr. and Mrs.) Man? What are their functions?

11) How does the architecture of the Temple facilitate our understanding of our own architecture? What is the basis?

12) How does Einstein's Theory of Relativity impact our understanding of immortality?

Group Discussion Questions: See *Small Group Leaders* section of this workbook.

Preparation for the Next Session:

Review the events of Day 1 through the 6th day. Read Genesis Chapter 2. Is the Sabbath Day for Christians? Why or why not?

Session 8:

Genesis

The Seventh Day
Chapter 2

> Thus the heavens and the earth were finished, and all the host of them.
>
> And on the seventh day God ended his work which he had made; and he rested on the seventh day from all his work which he had made.
>
> And God blessed the seventh day, and sanctified it: because that in it he had rested from all his work which God created and made.
>
> **Genesis 2:1-3**

Rabbinical View

- "…the Creator caused a repose to encompass the universe…"

  Maimonides, *The Guide for the Perplexed*, Part 1, Chapter 67

Thermal Decay

- Heat always flows from hot bodies to cold bodies.
- If the universe was infinitely old, the temperature throughout the universe would be uniform.
- It isn't; therefore, it isn't infinitely old.
- The universe had a beginning.
- And it is destined for an ending.

Roots in Eden

- "Clean" and "Unclean" — Gen 7:2,8
- The Kinsman-Redeemer — Gen 3:15
- Substitutionary Atonement — Gen 3:21
- The Sabbath — Gen 2:2,3

The Institution of the Sabbath

- The Sabbath becomes distinctive of Israel
  Ex 20:2, 8-11; Deut 4:13; 5:2-21
- Mosaic Laws concerning the Sabbath
  Ex 35:2,3; Lev 23:3; 26:34; et al;
  Isa 56:2,4,6; 58:13,14; Jer 17:20-22; Ne 13:19
  - Kindling a fire on the Sabbath was forbidden — Ex 25:3
  - The penalty for profaning the Sabbath by doing any work on it was death — Ex 31:14-17
- However,
  - Priests carried on their duties about the Tabernacle — Lev 24:8; Num 28:9, 10
  - The Temple was full of activities — 1 Chr 9:32; 23:31; 2 Chr 2:4; 8:13; 23:4; 31:3
  - The rite of circumcision was performed if it was the 8th day after the child's birth — Lev 12:3; Jn 7:22

The Exile

- Hosea predicted that God would make Israel's Sabbaths to cease because of her unfaithfulness   Hos 2:11
  - not meant to be permanent   Isa 66:23; Ezek 44:24; 46:1ff
- Nehemiah's reforms   Neh 13:15-22
  - many chose to die rather than desecrate the Sabbath, even for self-defense.   1 Macc 2:41
- However, as the rules multiplied, so did the ruses to circumvent them:
  You can't legislate devotion

Six Conflicts

1. He defended His disciples for plucking grain on the Sabbath by alluding to the time when David and his men ate the bread of the Presence   Mt 12:1-4; Mk 2:23-26; Lk 6:1-4
2. He also reminded His critics that the priests in the Temple profaned the Sabbath and were held guiltless   Mt 12:5
3. He referred to circumcising a male on the Sabbath day
     Lev 12:3; Jn 7:22, 23

Six Conflicts (con't)

4. Jesus expressed anger over those at Capernaum who showed more concern for the punctilious observance of the Sabbath than for a human being who was deprived of the use of a hand   Mk 3:1-5; Mt 12:8-14
5. Likewise, Jesus rebuked the ruler of the synagogue, who became indignant when He healed a woman who had a spirit of infirmity for 18 years   Lk 13:10-17
6. Jesus asserted His lordship over the Sabbath
     Mt 12:8; Mk 2:28; Lk 6:5

The Early Church

- The early Christians were loyal Jews;
  - they worshiped daily in the Temple at Jerusalem Acts 2:46; 5:42
  - they attended services in the synagogue Acts 9:20; 13:14; 14:1; 17:1, 2, 10; 18:4
  - they revered the law of Moses Acts 21:20
- The dispute over the requirements of a Gentile Christian were resolved at the Council at Jerusalem Acts 15

Paul and the Sabbath

- The Sabbath and festivals, are declared to be "only a shadow of what is to come" Col 2:16, 17
- To "observe days, and months, and seasons, and years" is to be slaves to "the weak and beggarly elemental spirits" Gal 4:9, 10; Col 2:20
- The observance of days is a characteristic of "the man who is weak in faith" Rom 14:1-6

Caveats about the "Early Church"

- **Lessons from the Seven Churches** Rev 2 & 3
  - Each was *surprised* by their report card:
    - Those that thought they were doing well weren't.
    - Those that thought they were not doing well, were.
- Many errors were rampant
  - Origen's allegorical hermeneutics
  - Augustine's Amillennialism, et al
- Furthermore, the rising anti-Semitism in the early church makes their views regarding the "Sunday Sabbath" suspect.

Constantine (274-337)

- He ultimately abolished
  - slavery,
  - gladiatorial fights,
  - the killing of unwelcome children, and
  - crucifixion as a form of execution.
- Frustrated with the paganism of the aristocracy in Rome, he relocated the capital of the world to Byzantium.

Sun Worship

- Constantine was faced with uniting an empire following 3 forms of pagan sun worship:
  - The Syrian solar cults of
    - *Sol Invictus* (the unconquerable sun)
    - *Jupiter Dolichenus* (the Roman storm god)
  - The Persian cult of
    - *Mithra*, the ancient Iranian god of light
- (This same pagan pragmatism Mohammed employed in syncretizing the 360 idols of Ka'aba into the worship of Al-Ilah in Islam.)

The Sunday "Sabbath"

- Only Christ has a right to make such a change
  Mk 2:23-28
  - As Creator, Christ was the original Lord of the Sabbath
    Jn 1:3 Heb 1:10
- It was originally a memorial of creation. A work vastly greater than that of creation has now been accomplished by him, the *work of redemption*.
- The entire Jewish calendar was changed at the Exodus, the birth of the nation Ex 12:2
  - We would naturally expect just such a change as would make the Sabbath a memorial of that greater work.
  - Yet, we can give no specific text authorizing the change

So Where are we?

- There are no grounds for *imposing* the Sabbath on the Christian, who is free from the burden of the law's demands. The Spirit of Christ enables him to fulfill God's will apart from the external observances of the law.
- The writer of Hebrews alludes to the Sabbath as a type of "God's rest," which is an inheritance of all the people of God

  Heb 4:1-11

  We are urged, in a larger sense, to "strive to enter that rest"...

The Trees in Genesis 2

And God said, Behold, I have given you every herb bearing seed, which is upon the face of all the earth, and every tree, in the which is the fruit of a tree yielding seed; to you it shall be for meat...
Genesis 1:29

and ending with

And out of the ground made the LORD God to grow every tree that is pleasant to the sight, and good for food; the tree of life also in the midst of the garden, and the tree of knowledge of good and evil.
Genesis 2:9

Marriage Instituted

- Christ based His teaching on this passage   Mat 19:3-9; Mk 10:2-12
  - quoted   Gen 1:27 and 2:23,24
  - One wife   Mat 19:8
  - heterosexual, permanent   Mt 19:4-6
  - male as the head   1 Cor 11:8,9; 1 Tim 2:13)

Genesis Session 8: The 7th Day

Genesis 2

1) Why do now believe the universe is *finite*? (What does thermodynamics have to do with it?)

2) Why do some believe the entropy laws were a result of the curse in Genesis 3?

3) Why was there no record of "evening" and "morning" on the 7th day?

4) How does Exodus 20:11 impact our views of "24-hour days" in Genesis?

___

5) How many of each animal did Noah take into the Ark? (How did he know?)

___

6) What *four* groups of worshippers were favored by the edicts Constantine regarding Sunday worship?

___

7) What is the role of Saturday during the millennium?

_____

_____

_____

_____

_____

_____

_____

_____

Group Discussion Questions: See *Small Group Leaders* section of this workbook.

Preparation for the Next Session:

Read Genesis Chapter 3. How is this chapter the "seed plot" of the entire Bible?

Session 9:

Genesis

The Seed Plot of the Bible
Chapter 3

> Now the serpent was more subtil than any beast of the field which the LORD God had made. And he said unto the woman, Yea, hath God said, Ye shall not eat of every tree of the garden?
>
> Genesis 3:1

נָחָשׁ *Nachash,* the Shining One
עָרוּם *aruwm,* wise, full of wisdom, prudent

Step 1: Introduce Doubt

> And the serpent said unto the woman, Ye shall not surely die:
> For God doth know that in the day ye eat thereof, then your eyes shall be opened, and ye shall be as gods, knowing good and evil.
>
> Genesis 3:4,5

Step 2: Denial

> Nevertheless death reigned from Adam to Moses, even over them that had not sinned after the similitude of Adam's transgression, who is the figure of him that was to come.
> Romans 5:14

Bases of Marriage

- Biological Basis
- Psychological Basis
- Sociological Basis
- Spiritual Basis

Prophetic Aspects of Marriage

- Akedah — Gen 22
  - Isaac and Rebecca — Gen 24
- Ruth & Boaz — Ruth
  - Kinsman-Redeemer (*Goel*)
    - Redemption of the Land
    - Gentile Bride
- YHWH and Israel — Hosea
- Church: Bride — Isa 62:5; 2 Cor 11:2; Rev 21:2; 22:17

"Gentile Brides"

Adam	Eve
Isaac	Rebekah
Joseph	Asenath
Moses	Zipporah
Salmon	Rahab
Boaz	Ruth

Adam as a "Type" of Christ

- "Son of God" — Luke 4:38
- Adam was not deceived — 1 Tim 2:14
- "Figure of Him…to come" — Rom 5:14
- Means of salvation to Eve
  - "Made sin" for her — 2 Cor 5:21
- Kinsman required — Rev 5
- Church = "Bride" — Isa 62:5; 2 Cor 11:2; Rev 21:2; 22:17

God Always Does the Seeking

- Adam
- Abraham, the idolater
- Jacob at Bethel, fleeing
- Moses, the fugitive in Midian

"Ye have not chosen me,
 I have chosen you" — John 15:16
The Shepherd always seeks the sheep

Genesis Session 9

When did "Israel" Begin?
1. As the "Seed of a Woman" Gen 3:15
2. From the Call of Abraham Gen 12
3. Through the Tribe of Judah Gen 49
4. Birth as a Nation Exodus 4
5. The Dynasty of David 1 Sam 7
6. The Virgin Birth Isa 7:14
- Summary: Rev 12

The Battle of the Seeds
- "Of Human Race?"
  - Cain & Abel Gen 4
  - Fallen angels corrupt mankind Gen 6
- Of Abraham's descendants?
- Of David's Dynasty?

The Stratagems of Satan
- Corruption of Adam's line Gen 6
- Abraham's seed Gen 12, 20
- Famine Gen 50
- Destruction of male line Ex 1
- Pharaoh's pursuit Ex 14
- The populating of Canaan Gen 12:6
- Against David's line 2 Sam 7

Genesis Session 9

Attacks on David's Line

- Jehoram kills his brothers — 2 Chr. 21
- Arabians slew all (but Ahazariah)
- Athaliah kills all (but Joash) — 2 Chr. 22
- Hezekiah assaulted, etc. — Isa 36, 38
- Haman's attempts — Est 3

New Testament Strategems

- Joseph's fears: — Matt 1; Deut 24:1
- Herod's attempts: — Matt 2
- Attempts at Nazareth: — Luke 4
- 2 storms on the Sea: — Mark 4; Luke 8
- The Cross
  - "Bruised for our iniquities" Isa 53
- Summary: — Rev 12

...and he's not through...

Bearing the Curse

- Ground cursed
  Made a curse
  Gal 3:13
- Man: eat sorrow
  Man of Sorrows
  Isa 53:3
- Thorns & Thistles
  Crown of Thorns
  John 18:8
- Sweat of brow
  Sweat as blood
  Luke 22:44

- Dust to return
  Dust of death
  Ps 22:15
- Sword barred
  Awake O Sword
  Zech 13:7
- Man to die
  "Why has thou forsaken me?"
  Ps 22:1; Mat 27:26

Fig Leaves

- Church-going
- Religious exercises
- Ordinances, Rules
- Philanthropy
- Altruism
- Personal Efforts

vs. Cross

Two Trees

- Cross ("tree") — Acts 5:30; 1 Pet 2:24
- Both in a Garden — John 19:41
- Curse linked to tree — Gal 3:13, 17
- Baker hanged — Gen 40:19
- Haman hanged — Esther 3:23

Contrasts

- Planted by God — Gen 2:9
  - Planted by man — Matt 27:35
- Pleasant to eyes — Gen 3:6
  - No beauty.. — Isa 53
- Forbidden
  - Commanded to eat
- Satan enticed
  - Satan prevents
- Brought Sin and death
  - Life and Salvation — John 6:53, 54
- Turned out of Paradise
  - Enters Paradise

Genesis Session 9: The Seed Plot of the Bible

Genesis 3

1) What does Matthew 19 & Genesis 3 teach about the nature and characteristics of marriage?

2) What was Satan's stratagems in getting "Mr. & Mrs. Man" to fall?

3) In what ways was Adam a prefiguring ("type") of Christ?

4) What are four basic aspects of the marriage union and describe the significant features of each.

5) Describe four examples in which the marriage union is used *prophetically*.

6) Review the major stratagems of Satan against the "Seed of the Woman" in Biblical history. How are they relevant to events of today?

7) Why are the entropy laws apparently linked to the curse in Genesis 3?

Group Discussion Questions: See *Small Group Leaders* section of this workbook.

Preparation for the Next Session:

Read Chapters 4 and 5. Find out all you can about Enoch.

Session 10:

Genesis

The 2nd Murder
Chapter 4

The Genealogy of Noah
Chapter 5

> So he drove out the man; and he placed at the east of the garden of Eden Cherubims, and a flaming sword which turned every way, to keep the way of the tree of life.
>
> **Genesis 3:24**

"God dwelt east of the Garden of Eden, between the Cherubim, as a tongue of fire, to keep open the way to the tree"

Jerusalem Targum

"The Way…"   Acts 9:2; 16:17; 18:25, 26; 19:9 et al

> And Abel, he also brought of the firstlings of his flock and of the fat thereof. And the LORD had respect unto Abel and to his offering:
>
> But unto Cain and to his offering he had not respect. And Cain was very wroth, and his countenance fell.
>
> **Genesis 4:4,5**

How did they know whether their offerings were accepted or not?

Fire from heaven?

- Moses & Aaron — Leviticus 9:24
- Gideon — Judges 6:21
- Samson's parents — Judges 13:20
- Elijah — 1 Kings 18:38
- David — 1 Chronicles 21:26
- Solomon — 2 Chronicles 7:1

> And to Jesus the mediator of the new covenant, and to the blood of sprinkling, that speaketh better things than *that of* Abel.
> — Hebrews 12:24

Representatively

- Both Cain and Abel from same parents
  - Fallen
- Both outside of Eden
  - Judicially alienated
- Differing Basis
  - His own works
  - vs. Completed work of Christ
- Death required
  - God would provide — Genesis 22:14

Typologically

Able	Jesus Christ
• A Shepherd	• The Good Shepherd
• Gave Offering	• John 10:1
• Hated by brother	• John 15:25
• Slain as enemy	• Acts 2:23
• Blood cries out	• Mark 12:9
• Firstling of flock	• 1 Peter 1:19
• Received witness	• Centurion, Satan/Judas, et al

Apostasy Begins

- "Then men began to *profane* the name of the Lord" Gen 4:25
- "…desisted from praying in the name"
  Targum of Onkelos
- "…surnamed their idols in the name"
  Targum of Jonathan
- Ascribes the origin of idolatry to the days of Enosh
  Kimchi, Rashi, Jerome, et al
  Maimonides, *Commentary on the Mishna,* 1168

Adam

אָדָם *adomah*, means "man."

Seth

שֵׁת *seth*, which means "appointed."

Eve said, "For God hath appointed me another seed instead of Abel, whom Cain slew." Genesis 4:25

Enosh

אֱנוֹשׁ which means "mortal," "frail," or "miserable."

It is from the root *anash,* to be incurable; used of a wound, grief, woe, sickness, or wickedness.

Kenan

קֵינָן which can mean "sorrow," "dirge," or "elegy."

Mahalalel

מְהָלֵל which means "blessed" or "praise"; and
אֵל El, the name for God.

"The Blessed God."

Jared (Yared)

יֶרֶד from the verb *yaradh,* meaning

"shall come down."

Enoch

חֲנוֹךְ which means "commencement,"
or
"Teaching."

Methuselah

מוּת *muth,* a root that means "death"

שׁלח *shalach,* which means "to bring," or "to send forth."

"His death shall bring."

Lamech

לֶמֶךְ a root still evident today in our own English word, "lament" or "lamentation."

"Despairing."

Noah

נֹחַ which is derived from *nacham,* "to bring relief" or "comfort,"

"Comfort, or Rest"

Genesis Session 10: The "Second" Murder

Genesis 4 - 5

1) When were the specifications for sacrifices given to man? How do we know?

2) Why did God replace the aprons with coats of skins?

3) How were the offerings of Cain and Abel different? Why was Cain's not accepted? How did he know?

4) List seven ways that Abel could be viewed as a "type" of Christ.

5) Where did Cain get his wife?

6) With whom did apostasy begin?

7) Summarize the hidden message in Genesis 5.

8) What was the first prophecy *uttered by a prophet* in the Old Testament? When was it uttered?

Group Discussion Questions: See *Small Group Leaders* section of this workbook.

Preparation for the Next Session:

Read Genesis 6. *Why* did God send the Flood? What did Jesus mean when He warned us, "*as the days of Noah were, so shall also the coming of the Son of man be*"? (Mt 24:37) Who were the "*Nephilim*"?

Session 11:

Genesis

The Days of Noah

Chapter 6

Jesus' Strange Warning

"But as the Days of Noah were, so shall also the coming of the Son of Man be."
— Matthew 24:37

What does that mean?

"Sons of God"

בְּנֵי־הָאֱלֹהִים *Bene HaElohim*

= angels

- OT: Job 1:6, 2:1, 38:7
- NT: Luke 20:36
- Book of Enoch
- Septuagint (LXX)

> And it came to pass, when men began to multiply on the face of the earth, and daughters were born unto them, that the (Sons of God saw the daughters of men) that they were fair; and they took them wives of all which they chose.
>
> Genesis 6:1,2

נֵי־הָאֱלֹהִים   *Bene HaElohim* "Sons of God"

בְּנוֹת הָאָדָם   *Benoth Adam* "Daughters of Adam"

The Nephilim

נְפִילִים   *Nephilim:* "the fallen ones"

נָפַל   *Nephal:* "to fall, be cast down to fall away, desert"

הַגִּבֹּרִים   *HaGibborim:* "the mighty ones"

Septuagint (Greek) LXX:

γίγαντες   *gigantes* (~ "giants?")

γίγας   *gigas* = "earth-born"

> These are the generations of Noah: Noah was a just man and (perfect in his generations), and Noah walked with God.
>
> Genesis 6:9

תָּמִים   *tamiym* = "without blemish, sound, healthful, without spot, unimpaired"

Genesis Session 11

οἰκητήριον *oiketerion,* habitation

Only Twice: Jude 6
2 Cor 5:2

> For in this we groan, earnestly desiring to be clothed upon with our house which is from heaven:
> 2 Corinthians 5:2

Genetic Discovery

- Scientists at Johns Hopkins University have discovered a gene in mice which controls growth: GDF-8
- Growth/Differentiation Factor-8 (GDF-8)
  - Disrupting GDF-8 yielded "supermice" three times larger and much stronger
    Nature, April 30, 1997

"Lines of Seth" View

- "Sons of God" ~ Sethite Leadership?
- "Daughters of Adam" ~ Daughters of Cain?
- Sin = failure to maintain separation?
- (*Nephilim* = ?)

Text Itself

- "Sons of God" *never* used of believers in the Old Testament
- Seth was not God; Cain was not Adam
- (No mention of the "daughters of *Elohim*")
- Grammatical Antithesis ignored
  – Psalm 81:1 - 6

Inferred Godliness of Seth

- *Only* Enoch and Noah's 8 spared
- "Took…wives" as "they chose"?
- Why did the Sethites perish in the flood?
- Enosh, Seth's son, *initiated* the defiance of God

Post-flood Nephilim

- "…also after that…"   Genesis 6:4
- *Rephaim, Emim, Horim, Zamsummim*
      Gen 14, 15
- Arba, Anak & his 7 sons (*Anakim*), encountered in Canaan: Num 13:33
- Og, King of Bashan: Deut. 3:11
      Joshua 12
- Goliath and his 4 brothers   2 Sam 21:16-22
      1 Chron 20:4-8

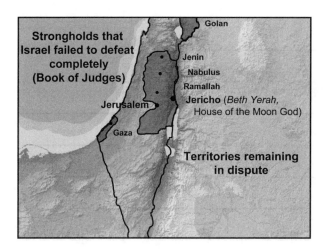

Strongholds that Israel failed to defeat completely (Book of Judges)

Territories remaining in dispute

Jericho (*Beth Yerah*, House of the Moon God)

The Nature of Angels

- Always appear in human form
  - Sodom and Gomorrah
  - Resurrection; Ascension
  - Spoke, took men by hand, ate meals
- Capable of direct physical combat
  - Passover in Egypt
  - Slaughter of 185,000 Syrians
- Don't marry (in heaven)
- [*Demons always seek embodiment*]

"habitation"

οἰκητήριον *oiketerion:* referring to the body as a dwelling place for the spirit.

Only twice in the Bible:

- Jude 6: from which the angels had "disrobed;
- 2 Cor 5:2: alluding to the heavenly body with which the believer longs to be "clothed."

Daniel's Visions Compared

	Daniel 2	Daniel 7	
Gold		Winged Lion	Babylon
Silver		Bear on side	Persia
Brass		Leopard	Greece
Iron		Terrible Beast	Rome I
Iron + Clay		10 Heads…	"Rome II"

What is the "Miry Clay?"

(Miry clay is clay made from mire, dust.)

And whereas thou sawest iron mixed with miry clay, they shall mingle themselves with the seed of men: but they shall not cleave one to another, even as iron is not mixed with clay.

Daniel 2:43

Genesis Session 11: The Days of Noah

Genesis 6

1) What characterized "the days of Noah"? In what way were they *prophetic*?

2) Who were the "Sons of God"? How do we know?

3) Who were the "daughters of Adam"? How is the designation important?

4) What is the significance of Genesis 6:1 & 6:2 being a single sentence?

5) Who were the *Nephilim*? How are they distinct from "fallen angels"?

6) How was Noah's genealogy free from "blemishes"?

7) Name three confirmations of the "angel view" of Genesis 6 in the New Testament.

8) Summarize the two locations of the term "*oiketerion*" in the New Testament and its apparent significance.

9) List at least 12 ways that the "lines of Seth" view is inconsistent with the Biblical record.

10) Contrast the characteristics of (fallen) angels and demons.

_____
_____
_____
_____

Group Discussion Questions: See *Small Group Leaders* section of this workbook.

Preparation for the Next Session:

Re-read Genesis 6.

Genesis Session 12

Session 12:

Genesis

The Flood

Chapter 7 & 8

Noah

- Mentioned as one of 3 righteous
  - with Job and Daniel — Ezek 14:14, 20
- Included in genealogies — 1 Chr 1:4; Luke 3:36
- New Testament References
  - Christ — Matt 24:37-39; Luke 17:26
  - Peter — 1 Pet 3:20; 2 Pet 2:5
  - Paul — Heb 11:7

Noah's Ark

300 cubits • 50 cubits • 30 cubits

Cubit = 18 inches   450 ft   75 ft   45 ft

Displacement: 24,000 tons?
- 1.4 million cu/ ft.
- 522 railroad cars
- 125,000 sheep
- 18,000 species

Genesis Session 12

Noah's Ark

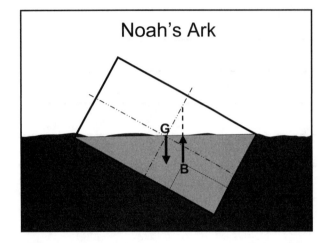

The Flood

Chapter 7

Other Flood Traditions

- Egyptian
- Babylonian
- Persian
- Greek
- Hindu
- Chinese
- Druids
- Polynesian
- Mexicans
- Peruvians
- American Indians
- Greenland

Universal or Local?

- Every living thing destroyed   7:4,23
- All high mountains under the entire heavens were covered   7:19
- Ark rested on the mountains of Ararat   8:4
- Promise: "never again"   9:11,15

Why?

- Dinosaurs quickly drowned and buried?
- Mammoths quickly drowned in North America, and quick-frozen in Siberia?
- Petrified forests found 100 miles from the South Pole by Admiral Byrd?
- Land animals found fossilized in locations below sea level?
- Sea animals found fossilized at high elevations?

Canopy Theory

- Atmospheric water shield protected the earth from cosmic radiation
  - Hence, longer lifetimes prior to the flood
- Water falls, complementing the subterranean waters unleashed   7:11
- Continental drift occurred from fractured land masses   10:25

The Genesis Record, Henry Morris and John C. Whitcomb, 1961

Geological Mysteries

- Grand Canyon origin
- Mid-Oceanic Mountain ranges
- Submarine Canyons
- Magnetic variations on ocean floor
- Coal and oil formations
- Frozen mammoths
- Metamorphic Rock
- Fossil graveyards
- Jigsaw fit of Continents

Hydroplate Theory

- Interconnected continents
- Subterranean water
- Increasing pressure(s)
- Horizontal buckling and eruptions

> Walt Brown,
> Center for Scientific Creation,
> Phoenix Arizona

The Flood

- Rained 40 days
- Not just rain: "fountains of the deep"
- Waters prevailed 150 days
- In the Ark 377 days
  - 5 months floating
  - 7½ months on the mountain

Chapter 8

The New Beginning

Months	Old	New
Tishri, (Ethanim)	1	7
Cheshvan, (Bul)	2	8
Chisleu	3	9
Tevet	4	10
Sh'vat	5	11
Adar	6	12
Nisan, (Aviv)	**7**	**1**
Ilyar (Zif)	8	2
Sivan	9	3
Tammuz	10	4
Av	11	5
Elul	12	6

New Beginnings

Crucified on the 14th of Nisan;
In the grave: 3 days;
Resurrection: 17th of Nisan
(the "7th month" of the Genesis Calendar)

Earlier Sightings

- Babylonian records
- Greek histories
- 275 B.C: Berossus, a Chaldean priest
- 30 B.C.: Hieronymous, the Egyptian
- 1st cent.B.C.: Nicholas of Damascus
- 70 A.D.: Josephus Flavius
- 350 A.D.: Epiphanius
- 1254: Haithon, Armenian King
- 13th century: Marco Polo references
- 1916: Russian Aviators; Czar interest; revolution interferes
- 1901-1904: George Hagopian
- 1952, 1955: Navarro visits; (Died in 1960).
- 1970's: Ed Davis, Ed Behling, George Jammal, et al
- February 20, 1993: CBS Prime Time Special, with photos

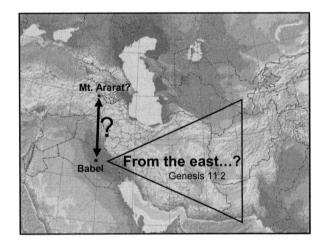

Mt. Ararat?
Babel
From the east...?
Genesis 11:2

	Event	Mon/Day	Ref.
	Noah enters the Ark	2 10	7:7-9
7 days	7 days later: rain begins	17	7:10-11
	40 days later: heavy rains stop	3 27	7:12
	110 days later: waters recede	7 17	7:24
150 days	Ark rests on Mr. Ararat		8:4
	74 days later: mtn tops visible	10 1	8:5
	40 days later: Raven sent;	11 11	8:6-9
	Dove #1 sent & returns	11 18	
	Dove #2 sent & returns with leaf	11 25	8:10
	Dove #3 sent; does not return	12 2	8:12
	22 days later: Water receded		
163 days	Noah saw dry land	1 1	8:13
57 days	Land completely dry; Ark exited	2 27	8:14-19
377 days		1 yr 17 days	

Genesis Session 12: The Flood

Genesis 7-8

1) Was Noah a real historical character? How do we know?

2) Did the flood really happen? How do we know? What evidences remain?

3) How many of each type of animal did Noah take into the ark? How did he know the distinctions?

4) Chart the 377 days on the ark.

5) What are the *prophetic* implications of Genesis 8:4?

6) What are some of the ecological changes in the post-flood world?

Group Discussion Questions: See *Small Group Leaders* section of this workbook.

Preparation for the Next Session: Read Chapters 9 & 10.

Session 13:

Genesis

The Post-Flood World
Chapter 9 & 10

A New Beginning
Genesis 9

- New Order
  - Not vegetarians anymore
  - Capital punishment ordained
  - Human government established
- Sinful man wiped out, but not sin
- Noah's Prophecy:
  "May God enlarge Japheth, And may he dwell in the tents of Shem; And may Canaan be his servant."

> Every moving thing that liveth shall be meat for you; even as the green herb have I given you all things.
>
> But flesh with the life thereof, *which is* the blood thereof, shall ye not eat.
>
> And surely your blood of your lives will I require; at the hand of every beast will I require it, and at the hand of man; at the hand of every man's brother will I require the life of man.
>
> **Genesis 9:3-5**

> Whoso sheddeth man's blood, by man shall his blood be shed: for in the image of God made he man.
>
> And you, be ye fruitful, and multiply; bring forth abundantly in the earth, and multiply therein.
>
> — Genesis 9:6,7

> I do set my bow in the cloud, and it shall be for a token of a covenant between me and the earth.
>
> And it shall come to pass, when I bring a cloud over the earth, that the bow shall be seen in the cloud:
>
> And I will remember my covenant, which *is* between me and you and every living creature of all flesh; and the waters shall no more become a flood to destroy all flesh.
>
> — Genesis 9:13-15

> And the bow shall be in the cloud; and I will look upon it, that I may remember the everlasting covenant between God and every living creature of all flesh that *is* upon the earth.
>
> And God said unto Noah, This *is* the token of the covenant, which I have established between me and all flesh that *is* upon the earth.
>
> — Genesis 9:16,17

Wine

- Nothing wrong   Deu 25:4; 1 Cor 9:7
  - Fermentation is a natural process
- Beneficial   Jdg 9:13; Ps 104:15; Prov 31:6; 1 Tim 5:23
- Symbol of blessings   Gen 27:28:37; Prov 9:2; Isa 25:6; Matt 26:28,29
- Blessed at Cana   John 2:9,10
- Drunkeness condemned   Prov 23:20; Isa 5:11, 22; Luke 21:34; Rom 13:13; 1 Cor 5:11; 6:10; Gal 5:21; Eph 5:18; 1 Thes 5:8

גָּלָה galah

- In Lev 18:6-19 all but one verse uses the causative form to indicate improper sexual behavior
- However, Noah had already uncovered himself, (the reflexive form) in v. 21.

Japheth

- **Gomer**: (Herodotus, Plutarch, et al): Cimmerians settled along the Danube and Rhine.
  - **Ashkenaz**: Germany.
  - **Riphath**: (Josephus: Paphlagonians; "Europe" from Riphath.)
  - **Togarmah**: Armenians, Turkey, Turkestan
- **Magog**: "Scythians" (Critical to understanding Ez. 38 & 39)
  - Hesiod, Greek didactic poet, 8th cent. B.C.
  - Herodotus, "The Father of History", 5th cent. B.C.

Japheth

- **Madai**: Medes (Kurds)
  - Emerged about 10th cent. BC; coalition with Persia (Elam), 7th cent BC.
- **Tubal**: Eastern Anatolia (Turkey)
- **Meshech**: Eastern Anatolia (Turkey)
- **Javan**: Ionia; Greece
- **Tiras**: Pelasgians of the Aegean; the Etruscans of Italy

Japheth

- Gomer
  - Ashkenaz
  - Riphath
  - Togarmah (Armenia, et al)
- Javan
  - Elishah
  - Tarshish (British Isles?)
  - Kittim
  - Dodanim

Nimrod

- "Rebel"
- First "World Dictator"
- Founder of Babylon & Nineveh
- (Detail in next session)

Ham

- **Mizraim:** Upper & Lower Egypt
  - Philistines ("Palestinians" = not sons of Ishmael)
- **Cush:** Ethiopia, Kassites, E of Assyria
  (Settled S of the 2nd cataract of the Nile)
  - Nimrod: Bab-El, Erech, Accad, Calneh
- **Phut:** (Settled W of Egypt) Ethiopia, N Africa
- **Canaan:** Sidon to Gaza, Sodom, & Gomorrah
  - Khittae ("Cathay")
  - Sinites (Sino = China)

Shem

- **Elam:** Persia (Iran)
- **Asshur**
- **Arphaxad**
  - Salah
    - Eber
      - Peleg ("earth divided")
      - Joktan
        - Reu — Gen 11:18f
        - Serug
        - Nahor
        - Terah
        - Abraham
- **Lud**
- **Aram**

Framework

- *Bene* ("the sons of") 12X
  vv.2-4,6-7,20-23,29,31-32
- *Yalad* ("he begot")   vv.8,13,15,21,25-26
- Canaan's descendants   vv.15-18
- Boundaries of Promised Land   v.19

The Table of Nations
Genesis 10

- 70 Nations from Noah
  - Ham
  - Shem
  - Japheth
- 70 Families
  - Entered Egypt   Gen 46:10
  - Bounds set   Deut 32:7, 8

The "Seventy"

Gen 46:26	66	Jacob
	4	Joseph / Manasseh / Ephraim
Gen 46:27	70	
	5	Joseph's grandsons (LXX)
Acts 7:14	75	

The Tower of Bab-El
Genesis 11

- One Language: Hebrew
- Godless Confederacy: 1st World Dictator
  - Nimrod – ("We will rebel")
- Plain of Shinar: Bab-El "Tower to Heaven"
  - Astrological Temple
  - Zodiac corrupted
- Tale of Two Cities
  - Babylon – the City of Man
  - Jerusalem – the City of God

Genesis Session 13: The Post-Flood World

Genesis 9 - 10

1) Summarize the arguments for a global (not regional) flood.

2) Summarize the post-flood changes in the global ecology.

3) Summarize the requirements (including non-Jews) for: a) abstaining from blood; b) capital punishment; c) abstaining from wine. Cite authorities.

4) Cite *two* places in the Bible that a "bow" is a token of a covenant.

5) Highlight the nations, and their Biblical relevance, represented by the following ancient tribal names:
   Japheth: Ashkenaz; Togarmah; Magog; Madai; Meshech; Tubal; and Javan
   Ham: Cush; Mizraim; Phut; and Canaan
   Shem: Elam; Aram; and Arphaxad

Group Discussion Questions: See *Small Group Leaders* section of this workbook.

Preparation for the Next Session:

Read Chapter 11. Also read Isaiah 13 & 14; Jeremiah 50 & 51; and Revelation 17 & 18. Is Babylon in Iraq relevant today? How?

Session 14:

Genesis

The Tower of Bab-El

Chapter 11

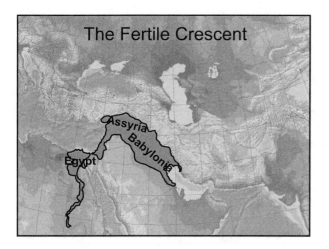

The Land of Nimrod

- Babel
- Accad (Akkad, Agade)
- Erech (Uruk, Sumeria)
- Nineveh (Assyria)
- Sumer (Shinar)
- Calah (20 mi from Nineveh)

> And the LORD came down to see the city and the tower, which the children of men builded.
>
> And the LORD said, Behold, the people *is* one, and they have all one language; and this they begin to do: and now nothing will be restrained from them, which they have imagined to do.
>
> Go to, let us go down, and there confound their language, that they may not understand one another's speech.
>
> Genesis 11:5-7

> So the LORD scattered them abroad from thence upon the face of all the earth: and they left off to build the city.
>
> Therefore is the name of it called Babel; because the LORD did there confound the language of all the earth: and from thence did the LORD scatter them abroad upon the face of all the earth.
>
> Genesis 11:8,9

Shem

- **Elam:** Persia (Iran)
- **Asshur**
- **Arphaxad**
  - Salah
    - Eber
      - Peleg ("earth divided")
      - Joktan
        - Reu
        - Serug
        - Nahor
        - Terah
        - Abraham *(Gen 11:18f)*
- **Lud**
- **Aram**

> And Terah took Abram his son, and Lot the son of Haran his son's son, and Sarai his daughter in law, his son Abram's wife; and they went forth with them from Ur of the Chaldees, to go into the land of Canaan; and they came unto Haran, and dwelt there.
>
> And the days of Terah were two hundred and five years: and Terah died in Haran.
>
> **Genesis 11:31-32**

> And Babylon, the glory of kingdoms, the beauty of the Chaldees' excellency, shall be as when God overthrew Sodom and Gomorrah.
>
> It shall never be inhabited, neither shall it be dwelt in from generation to generation: neither shall the Arabian pitch tent there; neither shall the shepherds make their fold there.
>
> **Isaiah 13:19,20**

> Therefore the wild beasts of the desert with the wild beasts of the islands shall dwell *there*, and the owls shall dwell therein: and it shall be no more inhabited for ever; neither shall it be dwelt in from generation to generation.
>
> As God overthrew Sodom and Gomorrah and the neighbour *cities* thereof, saith the LORD; *so* shall no man abide there, neither shall any son of man dwell therein.
>
> **Jeremiah 50:39,40**

Genesis Session 14

The Doom of Babylon

- **Destruction of Babylon** — Isaiah 13, 14; Jeremiah 50, 51
  - "Never to be inhabited"
  - "Building materials never reused"
  - "Like Sodom and Gomorrah"
- **Fall of Babylon** — 539 BC
  - Without a battle
  - Became Alexander's capital
  - Atrophied over the centuries
  - Presently being rebuilt
- **"Mystery Babylon?"** — Revelation 17-18

Destruction of Babylon

	Isaiah 13	Isaiah 14	Jeremiah 50	Jeremiah 51	Revelation 17	Revelation 18
Many Nations Attacking	4, 5	2, 26	2, 9, 41, 46	7	16	
Israel in the Land, Forgiven		1	4, 20			
Like Sodom & Gomorrah	19		40			
Never to be inhabited Bricks never reused	20	23	13, 26, 39	26, 29, 37		
During "Day of the Lord"	6, 10, 11, 13		25		√	√
Literal (Chaldean) Babylon	19	22	50	4, 24, 63		
King's fornication Drunk with wine				7	2	3, 9
Scarlet, purple Golden Cup				7	3, 4	6, 16

Genesis Session 14

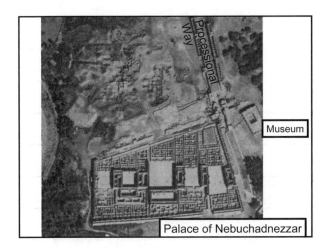

Mystery Babylon
Revelation 17 & 18

- The Great Whore 17
  - Rides the Beast with 7 heads, 10 horns
  - Mother of Harlots and Abominations
  - Drunk with the blood of the saints
- Babylon the Great (City) 18
  - Kings
  - Merchants
  - Those that trade by sea

The Woman in the Ephah
Zechariah 5:5-11

- Ephah
  - Woman called "Wickedness"
  - Sealed in with talent of lead
- Carried by two women
  - With wings of a stork
  - Between the earth and heaven
  - *"To build it a house in the land of Shinar: and it shall be established, and set there upon her own base."*

Genesis Session 14: The Tower of Bab-El

Genesis 11

1) Who was the first world dictator and where was his capital?

2) What was the origin of Babylon? What is its apparent role in the "End Times"?

3) What is the distinction between the "fall of Babylon" to the Persians in 539 B.C. and the "destruction of Babylon" as described in Isaiah 13 & 14 and Jeremiah 50 & 51?

4) Tabulate the similarities of these chapters with Revelation 17 & 18. How is this all relevant to our eschatological views?

5) How does the "woman in the ephah" (Zechariah 5:5-11) impact these views?

Group Discussion Questions: See *Small Group Leaders* section of this workbook.

Preparation for the Next Session:

Read Chapters 12-15: the Call of Abraham and the Abrahamic Covenant.

Session 15:

Genesis

The Call of Abraham
Chapter 12-15

Evidence of Design

- "Friend of God" — Prophetic Privilege
  - Abraham — James 2:23; Gen 18:17
  - Disciples — John 15:15
- "Beloved" — Apocalyptic Privilege
  - Daniel — Daniel 7-12
  - John — Revelation

Abraham (Highlights)

- Everlasting Covenant
- A struggle between the flesh and Spirit
  - Abraham's personal life
  - Ishmael vs Isaac;
  - Sarah vs Hagar; Gal 4:21-31
- Melchizedek
  - King and Priest of the Most High
- *Akedah*: Isaac offered Gen 22

Genesis Session 15

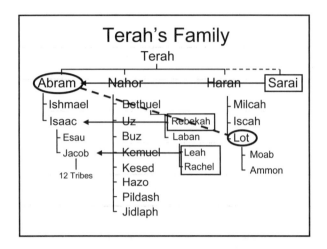

> Now the LORD had said unto Abram, Get thee out of thy country, and from thy kindred, and from thy father's house, unto a land that I will shew thee:
>
> And I will make of thee a great nation, and I will bless thee, and make thy name great; and thou shalt be a blessing:
>
> And I will bless them that bless thee, and curse him that curseth thee: and in thee shall all families of the earth be blessed.
>
> Genesis 12:1-3

> And he said, Men, brethren, and fathers, hearken; The God of glory appeared unto our father Abraham, when he was in Mesopotamia, before he dwelt in Charran,
>
> And said unto him, Get thee out of thy country, and from thy kindred, and come into the land which I shall shew thee.
>
> Then came he out of the land of the Chaldaeans, and dwelt in Charran: and from thence, when his father was dead, he removed him into this land, wherein ye now dwell.
>
> Acts 7:2-4

Genesis Session 15

> Now the LORD had said unto Abram, Get thee out of thy country, and from thy kindred, and from thy father's house, unto a land that I will shew thee:
>
> And I will make of thee a great nation, and I will bless thee, and make thy name great; and thou shalt be a blessing:
>
> And I will bless them that bless thee, and curse him that curseth thee: and in thee shall all families of the earth be blessed.
>
> **Genesis 12:1-3**

> So Abram departed, as the LORD had spoken unto him; and Lot went with him: and Abram *was* seventy and five years old when he departed out of Haran.
>
> And Abram took Sarai his wife, and Lot his brother's son, and all their substance that they had gathered, and the souls that they had gotten in Haran; and they went forth to go into the land of Canaan; and into the land of Canaan they came.
>
> **Genesis 12:4,5**

> And there was a famine in the land: and Abram went down into Egypt to sojourn there; for the famine *was* grievous in the land.
>
> And it came to pass, when he was come near to enter into Egypt, that he said unto Sarai his wife, Behold now, I know that thou *art* a fair woman to look upon:
>
> **Genesis 12:10,11**

Genesis Session 15

Anticipatory Parallel?

- The famine in the land Gen 12:10; 47:13
- The descent to Egypt to sojourn Gen 12:10; 47:27
- The attempt to kill the males but save the females Gen 12:12; Ex. 1:22
- The plagues on Egypt Gen. 12:17; Ex. 7:14-11:10
- The spoiling of Egypt Gen. 12:16; Ex. 12:35-36
- The deliverance Gen 12:19; Ex. 15
- The ascent to the Negev Gen. 13:1; Num. 13:17, 22

Is not the whole land before thee? separate thyself, I pray thee, from me: if **thou wilt take** *the left hand, then I will go to the right; or if* **thou depart** *to the right hand, then I will go to the left.*

And Lot lifted up his eyes, and beheld all the plain of Jordan, that it **was** *well watered every where, before the LORD destroyed Sodom and Gomorrah,* **even** *as the garden of the LORD, like the land of Egypt, as thou comest unto Zoar.*

Genesis 13:9,10

Then Lot chose him all the plain of Jordan; and Lot journeyed east: and they separated themselves the one from the other.

Abram dwelled in the land of Canaan, and Lot dwelled in the cities of the plain, and pitched **his** *tent toward Sodom.*

But the men of Sodom **were** *wicked and sinners before the LORD exceedingly.*

Genesis 13:11-13

Lot's Steps

Beheld
  Chose
    Departed
      Dwelt in the plain
        Pitched…toward
          Dwelt in Sodom
            Seated in the gate
              (Coucilman)

The Battle of 9 Kings
Genesis 14

Shemites
- Amraphel, king of Shinar
- Arioch, king of Ellasar
- Chedorlaomer, king of Elam
- Tidal, king of nations;

Hamites
- Bera, king of Sodom
- Birsha, king of Gomorrah
- Shinab, king of Admah
- Shemeber, king of Zeboiim
- King of Bela (Zoar)

- Served Chedorlaomer 12 years; 13th year rebelled
- Chedorlaomer defeated and spoiled the rebels
- Took Lot, Abram's nephew, captive from Sodom

The Slaughter of the Kings

- Abram's army (318 trained servants) rescues Lot, and the people of Sodom
- Melchizedek
  - King & Priest of Salem
  - Receives Abram's tithes   Heb 6:20
  - Allusions: Psalm 110; Hebrews 5, 6, 7
  - Administers Bread and Wine

Genesis 15

The Abrahamic Covenant

Unconditional Covenant
Genesis 15

A divinely ordered ritual:

barath, "To cut a covenant"
(Participants would divide a sacrifice, and together, in a figure "8," would repeat the terms of the covenant)

Here God goes it alone;
It is *unconditional*.

Three Major Promises

- God's Covenant with Abraham
  - In his seed all nations shall be blessed
- God's Covenant with the Nation Israel
  - If they faithfully served Him they'd prosper
  - If they forsook Him they would be destroyed
- God's Covenant with David
  - His family would produce the Messiah who would reign over God's people forever

Genesis Session 15: Abraham

Genesis 12-15

1) What does the title "Friend of God" signify?

2) Sketch Terah's family tree, and highlight the relevant links impacting the Biblical narrative.

3) How did Abraham *fail* to heed God's call? Why is it not more evident in the text?

4) List the ways that Abraham's events prefigured the bondage and deliverance of Israel generations later.

5) List the seven steps of Lot's backsliding.

6) What makes Melchizedek so distinctive? Why has he become a pivotal Biblical topic?

7) Why is the unconditional aspects of the Abrahamic covenant so relevant?

8) Map the extent of God's land grant to Abraham. How is that relevant to the geopolitical discussions today?

Group Discussion Questions: See *Small Group Leaders* section of this workbook.

Preparation for the Next Session:

Read Chapters 17 – 20.

Session 16:

Genesis
The Walk of Abraham
Chapters 16-20

Genesis 16
Hagar the Egyptian

"Angel of YHWH"

- Identified with Yahweh
  - Gen 16:13; 22:11-12; 31:11, 13; 48:16; Jud 6:11,16, 22; 13:22-23; Zech 3:1-2
- Yet distinct from YHWH
  - Gen. 24:7; 2 Sam. 24:16; Zech. 1:12
- May refer to a theophany of the preincarnate Christ
  - Cf. Gen. 18:1-2; 19:1; Num. 22:22; Jud. 2:1-4; 5:23; Zech. 12:8

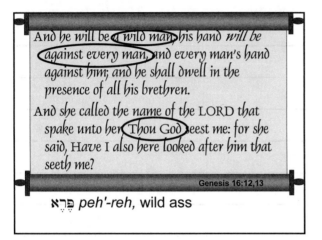

> And he will be *a wild man*; his hand *will be against every man*, and every man's hand against him; and he shall dwell in the presence of all his brethren.
> And she called the name of the LORD that spake unto her, *Thou God seest me*: for she said, Have I also here looked after him that seeth me?
>
> Genesis 16:12,13

פֶּרֶא *peh'-reh*, wild ass

Flesh vs. Spirit

- Abraham 430 years *before* the Law
  - Promises preceded the Law: cannot be disannulled
    - Galatians 3:17
- Ishmael vs Isaac
  - Two sons of two principles: Flesh; Spirit
  - Ishmael: of the flesh, in unbelief
    - "The son of the bondwoman will not be heir…"
  - Isaac: of promise, in response to faith
    - The Ultimate Triumph of Faith: the offering of Isaac
      - Galatians 4:21-32

Genesis 17

Circumcision Instituted
Son (Isaac) Promised
Names Changed

Genesis Session 16

Circumcision

- Vitamin K, clotting element, not formed until the 5th to the 7th day
- Prothrombin, also necessary
  - 3rd day: 30% of normal
  - 8th day: peaks at 110%, then levels off at 100% of normal
- How did Moses know to circumcise on the 8th day?   Gen 17:1

Papyrus Ebers
1332 BC

The well-stocked medicine cabinet:
- Lizard's blood
- Swine's teeth
- Putrid meat
- Moisture from pig's ears
- Milk goose grease
- Asses' hooves
- Animal fats
- Excreta from animals
  - Human, Donkeys, Antelopes, Dogs, Cats, Flies

Aleph א

= "First"; "Strength"; or "Leader"

Genesis Session 16

◺ Bet ב

- "House"; "Family"
- Beth Lehem; Beth-El; etc.

H Heh ה

(Hands lifted up; open window)

= "Behold"; "Revealed"
Also, "Breeze"; "wind;" "Spirit"

Names Changed
Genesis 17

אַבְרָם Abram

שָׂרַי Sarai

אַבְרָהָם Abraham

שָׂרָה Sarah

Genesis Session 16

Names Changed
Genesis 17

אַבְרָם	Abram
שָׂרַי	Sarai
אַבְרָהָם	Abraham
שָׂרָה	Sarah

He recognized Them

- Abraham hurried to them — v.2
  - He hurried back to the tent — v.6
  - He ran to the herd — v.7
  - his servant hurried — v.7
- Abraham bowed low before them — v.2
- He got water to wash their feet — v.4
- He served them
  - freshly baked bread — v.6
  - a choice calf — v.7 ⎤ Not Kosher?
  - curds and milk — v.8 ⎦
- He stood while they were eating — v.8; cf. vv.1-2

And the LORD said, Because the cry of Sodom and Gomorrah is great, and because their sin is very grievous;

I will go down now, and see whether they have done altogether according to the cry of it, which is come unto me; and if not, I will know.

And the men turned their faces from thence, and went toward Sodom: but Abraham stood yet before the LORD.

Genesis 18:20-22

Genesis 19

The Destruction of Sodom & Gomorrah

> But the same day that Lot went out of Sodom it rained fire and brimstone from heaven, and destroyed *them* all.
>
> Even thus shall it be in the day when the Son of man is revealed.
>
> In that day, he which shall be upon the housetop, and his stuff in the house, let him not come down to take it away: and he that is in the field, let him likewise not return back.
>
> Remember Lot's wife.
>
> Luke 17:29-32

Genesis 20

The Lapse at Gerar

Genesis Session 16: The Walk of Abraham

Genesis 16 - 20

1) List the reason that some identify the "Angel of the Lord" with: a) YHWH b) Distinct from YHWH c) Jesus Christ

2) Highlight the specific commitments that God gave Abraham in: a) Genesis 12 b) Genesis 15 c) Genesis 17

3) Why should a male infant be circumcised on the eighth day? What are the medical implications?

4) What was the significance of adding a "*heh*" to the names of Abram and Sarai?

5) What was the sin of Sodom?

6) What was the prerequisite condition for the angels to levy judgment on Sodom? What does this imply *prophetically?*

Group Discussion Questions: See *Small Group Leaders* section of this workbook.

Preparation for the Next Session:

Read Chapters 21, 22, & 24. How does Hosea 12:10 apply?

Session 17:

Genesis

Chapters 21, 22, 24

For it is written, that Abraham had two sons, the one by a bondmaid, the other by a freewoman.

But he *who was* of the bondwoman was born after the flesh; but he of the freewoman *was* by promise.

Which things are an allegory: for these are the two covenants; the one from the mount Sinai, which gendereth to bondage, which is Hagar.

Galatians 4:22-24

And the thing was very grievous in Abraham's sight because of his son.

And God said unto Abraham, Let it not be grievous in thy sight because of the lad, and because of thy bondwoman; in all that Sarah hath said unto thee, hearken unto her voice; for in Isaac shall thy seed be called.

And also of the son of the bondwoman will I make a nation, because he *is* thy seed.

Genesis 21:11-13

> And it came to pass at that time, that Abimelech and Phichol the chief captain of his host spake unto Abraham, saying, God *is* with thee in all that thou doest:
>
> Now therefore swear unto me here by God that thou wilt not deal falsely with me, nor with my son, nor with my son's son: *but* according to the kindness that I have done unto thee, thou shalt do unto me, and to the land wherein thou hast sojourned.
>
> Genesis 21:22,23

Genesis 22

The Offering of Isaac
The *Akedah*

Figures of Speech

- **Simile**: Resemblance Gen 25:25; Matt 7:24-27
- **Allegory:** Comparison by representation
  Gen 49:9; Gal 4:22, 24
- **Metaphor**: Representation Matt 26:26
- **Hypocatastasis**: an implied resemblance or representation Matt 7:3-5; Matt 15:13
- **Type**: A figure or example of something future Rom 5:14; Gen 22, 24
- **Analogy:** resemblance in some particulars between things otherwise unlike

Cosmic Codes, Appendix A

Genesis Session 17

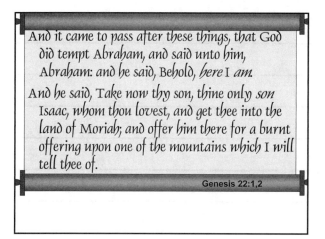

And it came to pass after these things, that God did tempt Abraham, and said unto him, Abraham: and he said, Behold, *here* I *am*.

And he said, Take now thy son, thine only *son* Isaac, whom thou lovest, and get thee into the land of Moriah; and offer him there for a burnt offering upon one of the mountains which I will tell thee of.

Genesis 22:1,2

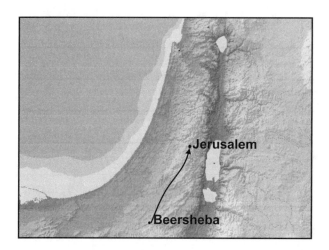

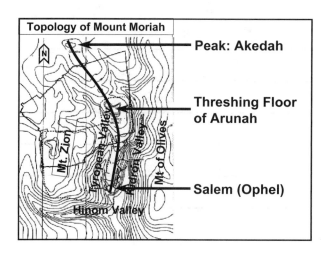

155

Genesis Session 17

> And he shall kill it on the side of the altar **northward** before the LORD: and the priests, Aaron's sons, shall sprinkle his blood round about upon the altar.
> — Leviticus 1:11

> And after this Joseph of Arimathaea, being a disciple of Jesus, but secretly for fear of the Jews, besought Pilate that he might take away the body of Jesus: and Pilate gave *him* leave. He came therefore, and took the body of Jesus.
> — John 19:38

not κεκρυμμένως   secretly (adverb)
     κεκρυμμένος   secreted (adjective)

Garden Tomb

- **General Charles George Gordon**
  - Commissioned as 2nd Lt., 1852;
  - Served in the Crimean War, 1853-56;
  - Distinguished himself in the Taiping Rebellion against the Manchu Dynasty, 1860;
  - Diplomatic and military engineering missions in England and Europe, 1864-74;
  - Governor of the Sudan, 1877
  - Served the British government in India, China, Mauritius and South Africa 1880-1883.
  - Discovered the Garden Tomb in Jerusalem in 1883.
- *Leviticus*, Andrew Bonar, 1846

(37 years earlier!)

> By faith Abraham, when he was tried, offered up Isaac: and he that had received the promises offered up his only begotten *son*,
>
> Of whom it was said, That in Isaac shall thy seed be called:
>
> Accounting that God *was* able to raise *him* up, even from the dead; from whence also he received him in a figure. Hebrews 11:17-19

Genesis 24
A Bride for Isaac

> The LORD God of heaven, which took me from my father's house, and from the land of my kindred, and which spake unto me, and that sware unto me, saying, Unto thy seed will I give this land; he shall send his angel before thee, and thou shalt take a wife unto my son from thence.
>
> And if the woman will not be willing to follow thee, then thou shalt be clear from this my oath: only bring not my son thither again. Genesis 24:7,8

Genesis Session 17

> And the man bowed down his head, and worshipped the LORD.
> And he said, Blessed *be* the LORD God of my master Abraham, who hath not left destitute my master of his mercy and his truth: I *being* in the way, the LORD led me to the house of my master's brethren.
> And the damsel ran, and told *them of* her mother's house these things.
>
> **Genesis 24:26-28**

> And Isaac came from the way of the well Lahairoi; for he dwelt in the south country.
> And Isaac went out to meditate in the field at the eventide: and he lifted up his eyes, and saw, and, behold, the camels *were* coming.
> And Rebekah lifted up her eyes, and when she saw Isaac, she lighted off the camel.
>
> **Genesis 24:62-64**

נָפַל *naphal*, be cast down, to fall prostrate before

Typology

- Abraham = The Father
- Isaac = The Son
- Eleazar = The Holy Spirit
  …sent to gather the Bride for the Son

Genesis Session 17

Genesis 21, 22, and 24

1) What does the name "Isaac" mean? Why?

2) Explain and give examples of Hosea 12:10.

3) List the prophetic parallels between Abraham's offering of Isaac and the Crucifixion of Christ on the Cross.

4) How do we know that Abraham *knew* that he was "acting out" a prophecy?

5) How does a single Greek letter reveal a major insight about Joseph of Arimathea?

6) Why did the cross need to be on the *north* side of the city? Why did Jesus' tomb need to be hewn out of a rock?

7) Why is the person of Isaac missing from the Genesis record from Gen 22:19 to Gen 24:62?

8) How do we know the *name* of Abraham's "eldest servant"? Why is that significant?

9) Summarize the *typological* parallels in Genesis 22 and 24.

10) What are the *prophetic* implications of the ancient Jewish wedding ceremony to our understanding of the end times?

_____
_____
_____
_____
_____
_____
_____
_____
_____

Group Discussion Questions: See *Small Group Leaders* section of this workbook.

Preparation for the Next Session:

Read Chapters 23, and 25 - 27.

Session 18:

Genesis

Chapters 23, 25, 26, 27

And Sarah was an hundred and seven and twenty years old: *these were* the years of the life of Sarah.

And Sarah died in Kirjatharba; the same *is* Hebron in the land of Canaan: and Abraham came to mourn for Sarah, and to weep for her.

Genesis 23:1,2

That he may give me the cave of Machpelah, which he hath, which *is* in the end of his field; for as much money as it is worth he shall give it me for a possession of a buryingplace amongst you.

And Ephron dwelt among the children of Heth: and Ephron the Hittite answered Abraham in the audience of the children of Heth, *even* of all that went in at the gate of his city, saying,

Genesis 23:9,10

Genesis 25
The Birth of Esau & Jacob

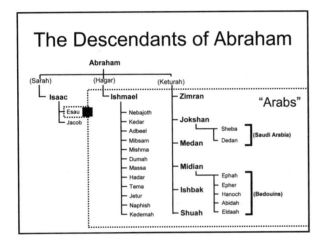
The Descendants of Abraham

> Then Abraham gave up the ghost, and died in a good old age, an old man, and full of years; and was gathered to his people.
>
> And his sons Isaac and Ishmael buried him in the cave of Machpelah, in the field of Ephron the son of Zohar the Hittite, which is before Mamre;
>
> The field which Abraham purchased of the sons of Heth: there was Abraham buried, and Sarah his wife.
>
> Genesis 25:8-10

Genesis Session 18

> And these *are* the names of the sons of Ishmael, by their names, according to their generations: the firstborn of Ishmael, Nebajoth; and Kedar, and Adbeel, and Mibsam,
> And Mishma, and Dumah, and Massa,
> Hadar, and Tema, Jetur, Naphish, and Kedemah:
> These *are* the sons of Ishmael, and these *are* their names, by their towns, and by their castles; twelve princes according to their nations.
>
> **Genesis 25:13-16**

Jacob

יַעֲקֹב *ya'aqob* "may He [God] protect"

עָקֵב *'aqeb* "heel"

עָקֹב *'aqob* "deceitful, sly, insidious"

Thus, "one who grabs the heel" or "one who trips up."

By-Pass of Firstborn

Seth	Cain
Shem	Japheth
Isaac	Ishmael
Jacob	Esau
Judah, Joseph	Reuben
Moses	Aaron
David	All his brothers

> And Jacob sod pottage: and Esau came from the field, and he *was* faint:
> And Esau said to Jacob, Feed me, I pray thee, with that same red *pottage*, for I *am* faint: therefore was his name called Edom.
> And Jacob said, Sell me this day thy birthright.
>
> Genesis 25:29-31

Genesis 26
The Covenant Confirmed

Parallels to Abraham

1. A famine — 12:10
2. A plan to go to Egypt — 12:11
3. The stay in Gerar — 20:1
4. Calling his wife his "sister" — 12:12-13; 20:2,11
5. The wife's beauty — 12:11,14
6. Abimelech's concern about committing adultery — 20:4-7
7. Abimelech's rebuke — 20:9-10

Genesis Session 18

> And the man waxed great, and went forward, and grew until he became very great:
>
> For he had possession of flocks, and possession of herds, and great store of servants: and the Philistines envied him.
>
> For all the wells which his father's servants had digged in the days of Abraham his father, the Philistines had stopped them, and filled them with earth.
>
> Genesis 26:13-15

Genesis 27
The Stolen Blessing

> And his mother said unto him, Upon me *be thy* curse, my son: only obey my voice, and go fetch me *them.*
>
> And he went, and fetched, and brought *them* to his mother: and his mother made savoury meat, such as his father loved.
>
> And Rebekah took goodly raiment of her eldest son Esau, which *were* with her in the house, and put them upon Jacob her younger son:
>
> Genesis 27:13-15

> And Isaac his father said unto him, Who *art* thou? And he said, I *am* thy son, thy firstborn Esau.
>
> And Isaac trembled very exceedingly, and said, Who? where *is* he that hath taken venison, and brought *it* me, and I have eaten of all before thou camest, and have blessed him? yea, *and* he shall be blessed.
>
> Genesis 27:32,33

"By faith Isaac blessed Jacob and Esau concerning things to come." Heb 11:20

Summary

- All participants were at fault:
  - Isaac attempted to thwart God's plan by blessing Esau!
  - Esau broke the oath he had made with Jacob
  - Rebekah and Jacob tried to achieve God's blessing by deception
    - Their victory would reap hatred and separation
    - Rebekah never saw Jacob again
  - Jacob alone did not destroy the family; parental preference did.

Ways to Study

- Archaeological   (Historical)
- Theological   (Doctrinal)
- Comparative   (Integral with NT, etc)
- Devotional   (Personal)
  - Observation   Who, What, Where, When
  - Interpretation Why, Primary implications
  - Application   So what: How me?

Genesis Session 18

Chapters 23, 25 - 27

1) List the people buried in the cave of Machpelah.

2) Why are the Saudi Arabians and the Bedouins *not* "sons of Ishmael"?

3) In what ways are the descendants of Esau and the descendants of Ishmael similar?

4) What does "Jacob" mean? How is it significant?

5) List the occasions that God bypasses the role of the "firstborn."

6) List the parallels between the narratives of Abraham and those of Isaac.

Group Discussion Questions: See *Small Group Leaders* section of this workbook.

Preparation for the Next Session:

Read Chapters 28 – 31.

Session 19:

Genesis

Chapters 28-31

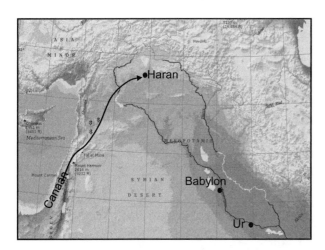

And thy seed shall be as the dust of the earth, and thou shalt spread abroad to the west, and to the east, and to the north, and to the south: and in thee and in thy seed shall all the families of the earth be blessed.

And, behold, I *am* with thee, and will keep thee in all *places* whither thou goest, and will bring thee again into this land; for I will not leave thee, until I have done *that* which I have spoken to thee of.

Genesis 28:14,15

Genesis Session 19

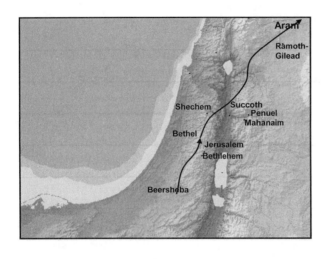

> And Laban had two daughters: the name of the elder was Leah, and the name of the younger was Rachel.
>
> Leah was tender eyed; but Rachel was beautiful and well favoured.
>
> And Jacob loved Rachel; and said, I will serve thee seven years for Rachel thy younger daughter.
>
> And Laban said, It is better that I give her to thee, than that I should give her to another man: abide with me.
>
> Genesis 29:16-19

> And he went in also unto Rachel, and he loved also Rachel more than Leah, and served with him yet seven other years.
>
> And when the LORD saw that Leah was hated, he opened her womb: but Rachel was barren.
>
> And Leah conceived, and bare a son, and she called his name Reuben: for she said, Surely the LORD hath looked upon my affliction; now therefore my husband will love me.
>
> Genesis 29:30-32

Genesis 30
Sons of Jacob

> And she said unto her, Is it a small matter that thou hast taken my husband? and wouldest thou take away my son's mandrakes also? And Rachel said, Therefore he shall lie with thee to night for thy son's mandrakes.
>
> And Jacob came out of the field in the evening, and Leah went out to meet him, and said, Thou must come in unto me; for surely I have hired thee with my son's mandrakes. And he lay with her that night.
>
> **Genesis 30:15,16**

The Patriarchs

```
                        Abraham
          ┌---------------┤
       (Hagar)         (Sarah)
       Ishmael          Isaac
                      (Rebecca)
                   ┌──────┤
                  Esau   Jacob
           ┌───────┬──────┬────────┐
        (Zilpah) (Leah) (Rachel) (Bilhah)
         Gad    Reuben  Joseph    Dan
         Asher  Simeon  Manasseh  Naphtali
                Levi    Ephraim
                Judah   Benjamin
                Issachar
                Zebulun
                                The 12 Tribes
```

Genesis Session 19

		In Egypt?
Reuben	Looked, affliction	Moses: Ex 2:25
		looked..affliction 3:7
Simeon	Hearing; Heard	"Heard my cry" Ex 3:7
Levi	Husband; joined	When was YHWH "joined?"
		Passover, Jer 31:31,32
Judah	Praise	Ex 5:11; Ps 106:11,12
		In Wilderness?
Dan	Judged; judgment	Wilderness: Meribah
Naphtali	Wrestlings; prevailed	At Amalek Ex 17:11
		In the Land?
Gad	Troop cometh	Nations oppose Israel
Asher	Happy	Overthrow
Issachar	Hire; service	Occupation
Zebulon	Dwelling	Occupation
		Kingdom?
Joseph	Adding	
Benjamin	Son of my right hand	

> I will pass through all thy flock to day, removing from thence all the speckled and spotted cattle, and all the brown cattle among the sheep, and the spotted and speckled among the goats: and *of such* shall be my hire.
>
> So shall my righteousness answer for me in time to come, when it shall come for my hire before thy face: every one that *is* not speckled and spotted among the goats, and brown among the sheep, that shall be counted stolen with me.
>
> **Genesis 30:32,33**

> And Jacob took him rods of green poplar, and of the hazel and chesnut tree; and pilled white strakes in them, and made the white appear which *was* in the rods.
>
> And he set the rods which he had pilled before the flocks in the gutters in the watering troughs when the flocks came to drink, that they should conceive when they came to drink.
>
> And the flocks conceived before the rods, and brought forth cattle ringstraked, speckled, and spotted.
>
> **Genesis 30:37-39**

Genesis 31

Jacob's Flight from Haran

The Nuzi Tablets

- 1925: 4000 clay tablets discovered E of Haran: 1500 BC
- Teraphim evidence of property ownership
  - Boundary marker as protection
- Sisterhood status misunderstood
- Surrogate motherhood by maidservants

And Jacob stole away unawares to Laban the Syrian, in that he told him not that he fled.

So he fled with all that he had; and he rose up, and passed over the river, and set his face *toward* the mount Gilead.

And it was told Laban on the third day that Jacob was fled.

Genesis 31:20-22

Genesis Session 19

> And she said to her father, Let it not displease my lord that I cannot rise up before thee; for the custom of women *is* upon me. And he searched, but found not the images.
>
> And Jacob was wroth, and chode with Laban: and Jacob answered and said to Laban, What *is* my trespass? what *is* my sin, that thou hast so hotly pursued after me?
>
> Genesis 31:35,36

Every thing that she lieth upon in her separation shall be unclean: every thing also that she sitteth upon shall be unclean. Lev 15:20

> Now therefore come thou, let us make a covenant, I and thou; and let it be for a witness between me and thee.
>
> And Jacob took a stone, and set it up *for* a pillar.
>
> And Jacob said unto his brethren, Gather stones; and they took stones, and made an heap: and they did eat there upon the heap.
>
> Genesis 31:44-46

> If thou shalt afflict my daughters, or if thou shalt take *other* wives beside my daughters, no man *is* with us; see, God *is* witness betwixt me and thee.
>
> And Laban said to Jacob, Behold this heap, and behold *this* pillar, which I have cast betwixt me and thee;
>
> This heap *be* witness, and *this* pillar *be* witness, that I will not pass over this heap to thee, and that thou shalt not pass over this heap and this pillar unto me, for harm.
>
> Genesis 31:50-52

Genesis Session 19

Genesis 28 - 31

1) Trace the reconfirmation of the Abrahamic Covenant through the sons of Abraham. Why is this important?

2) How was there ironic retribution in Laban's deceiving Isaac?

3) Explain the significance of the *Teraphim* and why were they important to Laban.

Group Discussion Questions: See *Small Group Leaders* section of this workbook.

Preparation for the Next Session:

Read Chapters 32 – 36.

Session 20:

Genesis

Chapters 32-36

Mahanaim: "Two Camps."

- "The angels of God" occurs only twice 28:12; 32:1
- *Zeh* ("this") is used four times 28:16-17
  - "This is the gate of heaven," 28:17
  - "This is the camp of God!" 32:2
- In both cases
  - Jacob interpreted what he had seen before naming it 28:17; 32:2
  - the identical expression is used in the naming of both places 28:19; 32:2
- *halak* and *derek* ("to go on one's way," "to take a journey") are used 28:20; 32:1

> And Jacob said, O God of my father Abraham, and God of my father Isaac, the LORD which saidst unto me, Return unto thy country, and to thy kindred, and I will deal well with thee:
>
> I am not worthy of the least of all the mercies, and of all the truth, which thou hast shewed unto thy servant; for with my staff I passed over this Jordan; and now I am become two bands.
>
> Genesis 32:9,10

> And he commanded the foremost, saying, When Esau my brother meeteth thee, and asketh thee, saying, Whose *art* thou? and whither goest thou? and whose *are* these before thee?
>
> Then thou shalt say, *They be* thy servant Jacob's; it *is* a present sent unto my lord Esau: and, behold, also he *is* behind us.
>
> Genesis 32:17,18

> And Jacob was left alone; and there wrestled a man with him until the breaking of the day.
>
> And when he saw that he prevailed not against him, he touched the hollow of his thigh; and the hollow of Jacob's thigh was out of joint, as he wrestled with him.
>
> And he said, Let me go, for the day breaketh. And he said, I will not let thee go, except thou bless me.
>
> Genesis 32:24-26

> And he said unto him, What *is* thy name? And he said, Jacob.
>
> And he said, Thy name shall be called no more Jacob, but Israel: for as a prince hast thou power with God and with men, and hast prevailed.
>
> And Jacob asked *him*, and said, Tell *me*, I pray thee, thy name. And he said, Wherefore *is* it *that* thou dost ask after my name? And he blessed him there.
>
> Genesis 32:27-29

Genesis Session 20

> And Jacob called the name of the place Peniel: for I have seen God face to face, and my life is preserved.
>
> And as he passed over Penuel the sun rose upon him, and he halted upon his thigh.
>
> Therefore the children of Israel eat not of the sinew which shrank, which is upon the hollow of the thigh, unto this day: because he touched the hollow of Jacob's thigh in the sinew that shrank.
>
> Genesis 32:30-32

Peniel

1. The wrestling occurred when Jacob was at the threshold of the land of promise
2. Jacob was named Israel — 32:28
3. The place name, Peniel, was given in response to Jacob's new name — 32:30
4. This story also results in a dietary restriction for the people of Israel — 32:32
   - Orthodox Jews still refuse to eat the tendon of the hindquarter of animals.

The Match

יַעֲקֹב   Ya`aqob ("Jacob")   the man

יַבֹּק   Yabboq ("Jabbok")   the place
          "emptying"

וַיֵּאָבֵק Ye'abeq ("he wrestled") the match

Before ya`aqob could cross the yabboq to the land of blessing, he had to ye'abeq [wrestle].

Genesis Session 20

> And Jacob said, Nay, I pray thee, if now I have found grace in thy sight, then receive my present at my hand: for therefore I have seen thy face, as though I had seen the face of God, and thou wast pleased with me.
>
> Take, I pray thee, my blessing that is brought to thee; because God hath dealt graciously with me, and because I have enough. And he urged him, and he took *it*.
>
> And he said, Let us take our journey, and let us go, and I will go before thee.
>
> **Genesis 33:10-12**

Genesis 34
Dinah Avenged

> And the sons of Jacob answered Shechem and Hamor his father deceitfully, and said, because he had defiled Dinah their sister:
>
> And they said unto them, We cannot do this thing, to give our sister to one that is uncircumcised; for that *were* a reproach unto us:
>
> But in this will we consent unto you: If ye will be as we *be*, that every male of you be circumcised;
>
> **Genesis 34:13-15**

Genesis Session 20

> The sons of Jacob came upon the slain, and spoiled the city, because they had defiled their sister.
>
> They took their sheep, and their oxen, and their asses, and that which *was* in the city, and that which *was* in the field,
>
> And all their wealth, and all their little ones, and their wives took they captive, and spoiled even all that *was* in the house.
>
> **Genesis 34:27-29**

Genesis 35
Jacob Returns to Bethel

> And God said unto him, I *am* God Almighty: be fruitful and multiply; a nation and a company of nations shall be of thee, and kings shall come out of thy loins;
>
> And the land which I gave Abraham and Isaac, to thee I will give it, and to thy seed after thee will I give the land.
>
> And God went up from him in the place where he talked with him.
>
> **Genesis 35:11-13**

Genesis Session 20

> And Israel journeyed, and spread his tent beyond the tower of Edar.
>
> And it came to pass, when Israel dwelt in that land, that Reuben went and lay with Bilhah his father's concubine: and Israel heard *it*. Now the sons of Jacob were twelve:
>
> The sons of Leah; Reuben, Jacob's firstborn, and Simeon, and Levi, and Judah, and Issachar, and Zebulun:
>
> Genesis 35:21-23

Genesis 36
Generations of Esau

> For their riches were more than that they might dwell together; and the land wherein they were strangers could not bear them because of their cattle.
>
> Thus dwelt Esau in mount Seir: Esau *is* Edom.
>
> And these *are* the generations of Esau the father of the Edomites in mount Seir:
>
> Genesis 36:7-9

Genesis Session 20

Genesis 32 - 36

1) Explain the *several* reasons for Jacob's naming the place "Mahanaim."

2) What did the wrestling event teach you about Jacob?

3) What was Jacob's strategy regarding his impending confrontation with Esau?

Group Discussion Questions: See *Small Group Leaders* section of this workbook.

Preparation for the Next Session:

Read Chapters 37 – 39. [And discover over 100 ways his story appears to prefigure the life of Jesus Christ!]

Session 21:

Genesis

Joseph
Chapters 37, 38, 39

Chapter 37

Joseph's Dreams

> And when his brethren saw that their father loved him more than all his brethren, they hated him, and could not speak peaceably unto him.
>
> And Joseph dreamed a dream, and he told *it* his brethren: and they hated him yet the more.
>
> And he said unto them, Hear, I pray you, this dream which I have dreamed:
>
> **Genesis 37:4-6**

Genesis Session 21

> And he dreamed yet another dream, and told it his brethren, and said, Behold, I have dreamed a dream more; and, behold, the sun and the moon and the eleven stars made obeisance to me.
>
> And he told *it* to his father, and to his brethren: and his father rebuked him, and said unto him, What *is* this dream that thou hast dreamed? Shall I and thy mother and thy brethren indeed come to bow down ourselves to thee to the earth?
>
> And his brethren envied him; but his father observed the saying.
>
> **Genesis 37:9-11**

> And his brethren went to feed their father's flock in Shechem.
>
> And Israel said unto Joseph, Do not thy brethren feed *the flock* in Shechem? come, and I will send thee unto them. And he said to him, Here *am* I.
>
> And he said to him, Go, I pray thee, see whether it be well with thy brethren, and well with the flocks; and bring me word again. So he sent him out of the vale of Hebron, and he came to Shechem.
>
> **Genesis 37:12-14**

> And Reuben heard *it*, and he delivered him out of their hands; and said, Let us not kill him.
>
> And Reuben said unto them, Shed no blood, *but* cast him into this pit that *is* in the wilderness, and lay no hand upon him; that he might rid him out of their hands, to deliver him to his father again.
>
> **Genesis 37:21,22**

> And they sent the coat of *many* colours, and they brought *it* to their father; and said, This have we found: know now whether it *be* thy son's coat or no.
>
> And he knew it, and said, *It is* my son's coat; an evil beast hath devoured him; Joseph is without doubt rent in pieces.
>
> And Jacob rent his clothes, and put sackcloth upon his loins, and mourned for his son many days.
>
> Genesis 37:32-34

Chapter 38

Judah's Sin With Tamar

Levirite Marriage

- (from Latin *levir*, "husband's brother")
- Codified in the *Torah* — Deut. 25:5-10
- The role of the *Goel*
  - The Kinsman-Redeemer — Ruth 1-4
  - The Ultimate Redemption — Rev 5

Genesis Session 21

> And he said, What pledge shall I give thee? And she said, Thy signet, and thy bracelets, and thy staff that *is* in thine hand. And he gave *it* her, and came in unto her, and she conceived by him.
>
> And she arose, and went away, and laid by her vail from her, and put on the garments of her widowhood.
>
> **Genesis 38:18,19**

> And it came to pass in the time of her travail, that, behold, twins *were* in her womb.
>
> And it came to pass, when she travailed, that *the one* put out *his* hand: and the midwife took and bound upon his hand a scarlet thread, saying, This came out first.
>
> And it came to pass, as he drew back his hand, that, behold, his brother came out: and she said, How hast thou broken forth? *this* breach *be* upon thee: therefore his name was called Pharez.
>
> **Genesis 38:27-29**

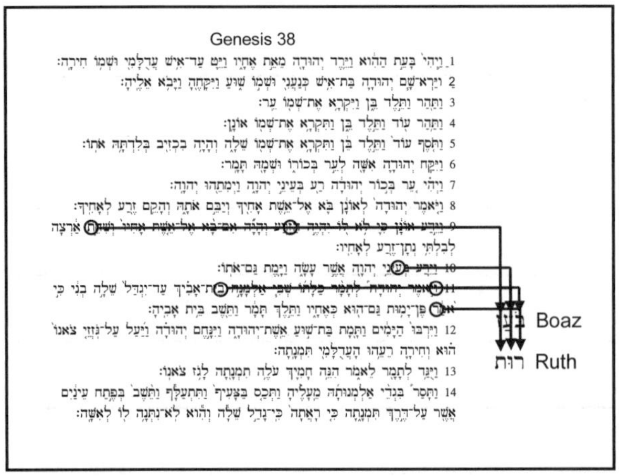

Genesis 38 (Hebrew text with diagram showing Boaz and Ruth / רות)

Genesis Session 21

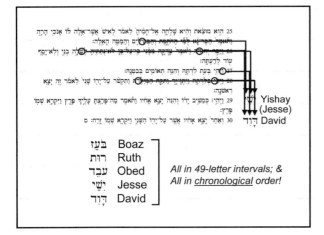

בֹּעַז	Boaz
רוּת	Ruth
עֹבֵד	Obed
יִשַׁי	Jesse
דָּוִד	David

All in 49-letter intervals; & All in chronological order!

The Book of Ruth
(Synopsis)

- "In the days the judges ruled…"
- The Ultimate Love Story
  - At the literary level
  - At the prophetic, personal level
- One of the most significant books for *the Church*
  - The Role of the Kinsman-Redeemer
  - Essential Pre-requisite to Revelation

Ruth Gleaning
Chapter 2

- The Law of Gleaning Lev 19:9,10; Deut 24:19-2
  - Provision for the Destitute
- "Happens" upon the field of Boaz
  - Boaz = "In Him is Strength" (Temple Pillar)
  - Introduced by "Unnamed Servant"
  - Protection + "Handfuls on purpose…"
- *Goel*: Kinsman-Redeemer
  - Law of Redemption Lev 25:47-50
  - Law of Levirite Marriage Deut 25:5-10

The Threshing Floor
Chapter 3

- Naomi recognizes an opportunity
  - For the redemption of her land
  - For a new life for Ruth
  - She instructs Ruth on what to do
- Ruth approaches Boaz
  - To fulfill the role of a *Goel*
- A "nearer kinsman" in the way . . .
- (6 measures of barley = a code for Naomi)

Observations

- In order to bring Ruth to Naomi, Naomi had to be exiled from her land.
- What the Law could not do, Grace did.
- Ruth does not replace Naomi.
- Ruth learns of Boaz's ways thru Naomi.
- Naomi meets Boaz thru Ruth.
- No matter how much Boaz loved Ruth, he had to await *her* move.
- Boaz, not Ruth, confronts the "Nearer Kinsman."

Chapter 39

Joseph Imprisoned

Genesis Session 21: Joseph

Genesis 37 - 39

1) How was Joseph's special coat *prophetic*?

2) How does Jacob's reaction to Joseph's second dream impact your understanding of Revelation 12?

3) Why were the slave traders *not* "Ishmaelites" in the denotative sense?

4) List the parallels in the deception of Jacob and the earlier deception of Isaac.

_____

5) List the occasions where the order of the "firstborn" is by-passed in God's plans.

_____

6) Contrast the genealogies hidden in Gen 38 with those listed in the Book of Ruth.

_____

7) What is the role of the *goel?* What are the requirements for him?

_____

8) Where else is the Holy Spirit usually prefigured (in a "type") as an unnamed servant? Why?

9) What *two* times was Joseph's clothing used to spread a false report about him?

Group Discussion Questions: See *Small Group Leaders* section of this workbook.

Preparation for the Next Session:

Read the entire story of Joseph: Chapters 37 – 49. Also, read Psalm 105.

Session 22:

Genesis

Joseph in Egypt

Chapters 40 - 45

And Joseph came in unto them in the morning, and looked upon them, and, behold, they *were* sad.

And he asked Pharaoh's officers that *were* with him in the ward of his lord's house, saying, Wherefore look ye *so* sadly to day?

And they said unto him, We have dreamed a dream, and *there is* no interpreter of it. And Joseph said unto them, *Do* not interpretations *belong* to God? tell me *them*, I pray you.

Genesis 40:6-8

When the chief baker saw that the interpretation was good, he said unto Joseph, I also *was* in my dream, and, behold, *I had* three white baskets on my head:

And in the uppermost basket *there was* of all manner of bakemeats for Pharaoh; and the birds did eat them out of the basket upon my head.

Genesis 40:16,17

Genesis Session 22

> And it came to pass the third day, *which was* Pharaoh's birthday, that he made a feast unto all his servants: and he lifted up the head of the chief butler and of the chief baker among his servants.
>
> And he restored the chief butler unto his butlership again; and he gave the cup into Pharaoh's hand:
>
> **Genesis 40:20,21**

Bread & Wine

- First mention: Melchizedek administers to Abraham — Gen 14
- The Baker & Wine Steward — Gen 40
- The Lord's Last Supper — Matt 26
- Communion — 1 Cor 11

> And *there was* there with us a young man, an Hebrew, servant to the captain of the guard; and we told him, and he interpreted to us our dreams; to each man according to his dream he did interpret.
>
> And it came to pass, as he interpreted to us, so it was; me he restored unto mine office, and him he hanged.
>
> **Genesis 41:12,13**

Genesis Session 22

> And the plenty shall not be known in the land by reason of that famine following; for it *shall be* very grievous.
>
> And for that the dream was doubled unto Pharaoh twice; *it is* because the thing *is* established by God, and God will shortly bring it to pass.
>
> Now therefore let Pharaoh look out a man discreet and wise, and set him over the land of Egypt.
>
> **Genesis 41:31-33**

> And Pharaoh said unto Joseph, Forasmuch as God hath shewed thee all this, *there is* none so discreet and wise as thou *art*:
>
> Thou shalt be over my house, and according unto thy word shall all my people be ruled: only in the throne will I be greater than thou.
>
> **Genesis 41:39,40**

> And in the seven plenteous years the earth brought forth by handfuls.
>
> And he gathered up all the food of the seven years, which were in the land of Egypt, and laid up the food in the cities: the food of the field, which *was* round about every city, laid he up in the same.
>
> And Joseph gathered corn as the sand of the sea, very much, until he left numbering; for *it was* without number.
>
> **Genesis 41:47-49**

Chapter 42

The Move to Egypt
Brother's 1st Visit

> And Joseph said unto them, That *is it* that I spake unto you, saying, Ye *are* spies:
>
> Hereby ye shall be proved: By the life of Pharaoh ye shall not go forth hence, except your youngest brother come hither.
>
> Send one of you, and let him fetch your brother, and ye shall be kept in prison, that your words may be proved, whether *there be any* truth in you: or else by the life of Pharaoh surely ye *are* spies.
>
> Genesis 42:14-16

> And the man, the lord of the country, said unto us, Hereby shall I know that ye *are* true *men*; leave one of your brethren *here* with me, and take *food for* the famine of your households, and be gone:
>
> And bring your youngest brother unto me: then shall I know that ye *are* no spies, but *that* ye *are* true *men: so* will I deliver you your brother, and ye shall traffick in the land.
>
> Genesis 42:33,34

Genesis Session 22

> I will be surety for him; of my hand shalt thou require him: if I bring him not unto thee, and set him before thee, then let me bear the blame for ever:
>
> For except we had lingered, surely now we had returned this second time.
>
> **Genesis 43:9,10**

> And the man brought the men into Joseph's house, and gave *them* water, and they washed their feet; and he gave their asses provender.
>
> And they made ready the present against Joseph came at noon: for they heard that they should eat bread there.
>
> And when Joseph came home, they brought him the present which *was* in their hand into the house, and bowed themselves to him to the earth.
>
> **Genesis 43:24-26**

> And they said unto him, Wherefore saith my lord these words? God forbid that thy servants should do according to this thing:
>
> Behold, the money, which we found in our sacks' mouths, we brought again unto thee out of the land of Canaan: how then should we steal out of thy lord's house silver or gold?
>
> With whomsoever of thy servants it be found, both let him die, and we also will be my lord's bondmen.
>
> **Genesis 44:7-9**

Genesis Session 22

> Then Judah came near unto him, and said, Oh my lord, let thy servant, I pray thee, speak a word in my lord's ears, and let not thine anger burn against thy servant: for thou *art* even as Pharaoh.
>
> My lord asked his servants, saying, Have ye a father, or a brother?
>
> — Genesis 44:18,19

"The most complete pattern of genuine natural eloquence extant in any language."
— Sir Walter Scott

> Then Joseph could not refrain himself before all them that stood by him; and he cried, Cause every man to go out from me. And there stood no man with him, while Joseph made himself known unto his brethren.
>
> And he wept aloud: and the Egyptians and the house of Pharaoh heard.
>
> And Joseph said unto his brethren, I *am* Joseph; doth my father yet live? And his brethren could not answer him; for they were troubled at his presence.
>
> — Genesis 45:1-3

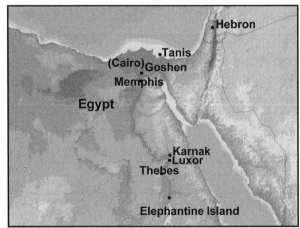

202

Genesis Session 22: Joseph in Egypt

Genesis 40 - 45

1) Contrast the details of the two dreams that Joseph interpreted while in prison.

2) What is the possible significance of the detail that the bread in the baker's dream may have had "holes" in it?

3) How long did he have to wait after the butler was released?

4) Why do we suspect that Joseph had been held in the cistern for three days?

5) Compare the careers of Joseph and Daniel: similarities and differences.

6) Compare the narratives of Jacob and Joseph: similarities and differences.

Group Discussion Questions: See *Small Group Leaders* section of this workbook.

Preparation for the Next Session:

Re-read the career of Joseph, and focus on chapters 46 – 48. Also read chapter 50. (We will defer chapter 49 until our final session.)

Session 23:

Genesis

The Family in Egypt

Chapters 46 – 48, 50

Chapter 46

Jacob Journeys to Egypt

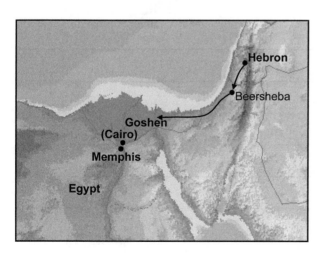

> And the sons of Dan; Hushim.
>
> And the sons of Naphtali; Jahzeel, and Guni, and Jezer, and Shillem.
>
> These *are* the sons of Bilhah, which Laban gave unto Rachel his daughter, and she bare these unto Jacob: all the souls *were* seven.
>
> **Genesis 46:23-25**

Reconciliation

(verse)		
(15)	Leah's children and grandchildren	33
(18)	Zilpah's children and grandchildren	16
(22)	Rachel's children and grandchildren	14
(25)	Bilhah's children and grandchildren	7
		70
(15)	Dinah	+ 1
		71
(12)	(Er and Onan died in Canaan)	
(20)	Joseph & his two sons, already in Egypt	- 5
(26)	Those who went to Egypt with Jacob	66
(27)	Joseph, Manasseh, Ephraim, Jacob	+ 4
(27)	Jacob and his progeny in Egypt	70

> And Joseph said unto his brethren, and unto his father's house, I will go up, and shew Pharaoh, and say unto him, My brethren, and my father's house, which *were* in the land of Canaan, are come unto me;
>
> And the men *are* shepherds, for their trade hath been to feed cattle; and they have brought their flocks, and their herds, and all that they have.
>
> **Genesis 46:31,32**

> And Pharaoh said unto Jacob, How old *art* thou?
>
> And Jacob said unto Pharaoh, The days of the years of my pilgrimage *are* an hundred and thirty years: few and evil have the days of the years of my life been, and have not attained unto the days of the years of the life of my fathers in the days of their pilgrimage.
>
> And Jacob blessed Pharaoh, and went out from before Pharaoh.
>
> **Genesis 47:8-10**

> And Joseph placed his father and his brethren, and gave them a possession in the land of Egypt, in the best of the land, in the land of Rameses, as Pharaoh had commanded.
>
> And Joseph nourished his father, and his brethren, and all his father's household, with bread, according to *their* families.
>
> And *there was* no bread in all the land; for the famine *was* very sore, so that the land of Egypt and *all* the land of Canaan fainted by reason of the famine.
>
> **Genesis 47:11-13**

> Then Joseph said unto the people, Behold, I have bought you this day and your land for Pharaoh: lo, *here is* seed for you, and ye shall sow the land.
>
> And it shall come to pass in the increase, that ye shall give the fifth *part* unto Pharaoh, and four parts shall be your own, for seed of the field, and for your food, and for them of your households, and for food for your little ones.
>
> **Genesis 47:23,24**

> And it came to pass after these things, that *one* told Joseph, Behold, thy father *is* sick: and he took with him his two sons, Manasseh and Ephraim.
>
> And *one* told Jacob, and said, Behold, thy son Joseph cometh unto thee: and Israel strengthened himself, and sat upon the bed.
>
> **Genesis 48:1,2**

> And Israel said unto Joseph, I had not thought to see thy face: and, lo, God hath shewed me also thy seed.
>
> And Joseph brought them out from between his knees, and he bowed himself with his face to the earth.
>
> And Joseph took them both, Ephraim in his right hand toward Israel's left hand, and Manasseh in his left hand toward Israel's right hand, and brought *them* near unto him.
>
> **Genesis 48:11-13**

> And Israel said unto Joseph, Behold, I die: but God shall be with you, and bring you again unto the land of your fathers.
>
> Moreover I have given to thee one portion above thy brethren, which I took out of the hand of the Amorite with my sword and with my bow.
>
> **Genesis 48:21,22**

Genesis Session 23

> And when the days of his mourning were past, Joseph spake unto the house of Pharaoh, saying, If now I have found grace in your eyes, speak, I pray you, in the ears of Pharaoh, saying,
>
> My father made me swear, saying, Lo, I die: in my grave which I have digged for me in the land of Canaan, there shalt thou bury me. Now therefore let me go up, I pray thee, and bury my father, and I will come again.
>
> Genesis 50:4,5

> And Pharaoh said, Go up, and bury thy father, according as he made thee swear.
>
> And Joseph went up to bury his father: and with him went up all the servants of Pharaoh, the elders of his house, and all the elders of the land of Egypt,
>
> And all the house of Joseph, and his brethren, and his father's house: only their little ones, and their flocks, and their herds, they left in the land of Goshen.
>
> Genesis 50:6-8

> And when Joseph's brethren saw that their father was dead, they said, Joseph will peradventure hate us, and will certainly requite us all the evil which we did unto him.
>
> And they sent a messenger unto Joseph, saying, Thy father did command before he died, saying,
>
> Genesis 50:15,16

> And Joseph said unto his brethren, I die: and God will surely visit you, and bring you out of this land unto the land which he sware to Abraham, to Isaac, and to Jacob.
>
> And Joseph took an oath of the children of Israel, saying, God will surely visit you, and ye shall carry up my bones from hence.
>
> So Joseph died, *being* an hundred and ten years old: and they embalmed him, and he was put in a coffin in Egypt.
>
> **Genesis 50:24-26**

Joseph as a Type of Christ

37:2	Occupation: Shepherd	Ps 23
	(Abel, Jacob, Joseph, Moses, David)	
37:3	Vestment Distinctive	Ps 22:18; Matt 27:35
37:4	Hatred of his brethren	Jn 1:11
	Because of Who He Was	Jn 5:18; 6:41 10:30,31
		1 Cor 16:22 Psa 2:12
	Hated because of his words	Jn 7:7; 8:40
37:7	Future sovereignty foretold	Mt 26:64
37:13	Sent forth by his father	1 Jn 4:10; Heb 10:7
37:17	Seeks until he finds	Mk 9:8

Joseph as a Type of Christ

41:33-36	Wonderful Counselor	Col 2:3
41:40-43	Seated on the throne of another	Rev 3:21
	[Distinction between Father's & Son's thrones]	
41:38	Exalted because of personal worthiness and service	Phil 2:6-9
41:45	Has a wife (Gentile) given to him	Rev 19:7-8
41:46	30 years old when began work	Lk 3:23
41:55	Dispenses the Bread of Life	Acts 4:12; Jn 6:26f; 14:6
42:1f	Brethren driven out of own land	Gen 15:13; Deut 28:63f
42:6, 8	Unknown & unrecognized by brethren	Jn 1:11
	7 years: Jacob's Trouble	Jer 30:7; Dan 12:1; Mk 13:19, 20; Amos 8:11,12; Isa 55:6; Jer 8:20; Rev 3:10

[Over 100 listed in our supplemental notes]

Genesis Session 23: The Family in Egypt

Genesis 46 - 48, 50

1) Reconcile the numbers of Jacob's family traveling to Egypt (Gen 46:26, 27).

2) What was the significance of Jacob's adoption of Joseph's two children as his own?

3) What might have been the impact if Jacob had *not* adopted Joseph's two sons?

Group Discussion Questions: See *Small Group Leaders* section of this workbook.

Preparation for the Next Session:

Read (carefully) Chapter 49 and *also* Deuteronomy 33. And also be prepared for some surprises…

Genesis Session 24

Session 24:

Genesis

The Tribes Prophetically
Chapter 49

The 12 Tribes

Leah:
- Gen 29:32 Reuben "Behold a son"
- Gen 29:33 Simeon "Heard"
- Gen 29:34 Levi "Joined to"
- Gen 29:35 Judah "Praise"

Bilhah: (Rachel)
- Gen 30:6 Dan "Judge"
- Gen 30:8 Naphtali "Wrestling;" "Struggles"

Zilpah: (Leah)
- Gen 30:11 Gad "Troop;" "fortune"
- Gen 30:13 Asher "Happy"

Leah:
- Gen 30:18 Issachar "Recompense"
- Gen 30:20 Zebulun "Exalted"

Rachel:
- Gen 30:24 Joseph "YHWH has added"
- Gen 35:18 Benjamin "Son of the right hand"

And this *is* the blessing, wherewith Moses the man of God blessed the children of Israel before his death.

And he said, The LORD came from Sinai, and rose up from Seir unto them; he shined forth from mount Paran, and he came with ten thousands of saints: from his right hand *went* a fiery law for them.

Deuteronomy 33:1,2

Closing the *Torah*, Moses did likewise

Reuben

- The firstborn of Jacob by Leah Gen 29:32
- The name is connected with the phrase, "the Lord has looked upon my affliction."
- His incestuous act with Bilhah, his father's concubine Gen 35:22;
- It was Reuben who advised his brothers not to kill Joseph, and returned to the pit to release him Gen 37:21, 29
- Reuben's forfeited birthright given to Joseph 1 Chr 5:1,2
- The tribe of Reuben was involved in the rebellion in the wilderness Num 16:1

Levi

- Name לֵוִי is linked with the root "to join"
- Avenged the seduction of Dinah Gen. 34; 49:5-7
- Zeal against idolatry a cause of their appointment Ex 32:26-28; Deut 33:9,10; Mal 2:4,5
- Exempt from enrollment for military duty Num 1:47-54, with 1 Chr 12:26
- Subordinate to the sons of Aaron Num 3:9; 8:19; 18:6
- Teachers of the law Deut 33:10; 2 Chr 17:8,9; 30:22; 35:3
- Were judges Deut 17:9; 1 Chr 23:4; 26:29; 2 Chr 19:8-11
- Guarded king's person and house in times of danger 2 Kgs 11:5-9; 2 Chr 23:5-7

Simeon

- 2nd son of Jacob by Leah Gen 29:33
- Associated with Levi in the terrible act of vengeance against Hamor and the Shechemites Gen 34:25,26
- Detained by Joseph in Egypt as a hostage Gen 42:24
- His father, when dying, pronounced a malediction against him; to be "divided and scattered" Gen 49:5-7
    - Decreased in the wilderness by 2/3 Num 1:23 26:14
    - Dwindled in number; sank into insignificance
- Moses pronounces no blessing on this tribe.
- They didn't lose their identity:
    - 13 Simeonite princes in days of Hezekiah 1 Chr 4:34-38

Sceptre Departs

- Herod the Great died (4 BC?)
  - (Herod Antipater: murdered)
  - Herod Archelaus
    - Appointed "Entharch" by Caesar Augustus
    - Dethroned, Banished (6-7 AD)
  - Caponius appointed Procurator
    - Transfer of power *Josephus, Antiquities* 20:9
- Priests officially mourned
  - *"Woe unto us for the scepter has departed from Judah and the Messiah has not come!"*
    Jerusalem Talmud, Sanhedrin, f.24

Judah

- Name means "praised," root הדי, "to praise." Gen 49:8
- Intercedes for Joseph's life when brethren were about to slay him; proposes sale to the Ishmaelites, Gen. 37:26,27
- Incest with Tamar, his daughter-in-law Gen. 38:12-26
- Loyal to the house of David at the time of the revolt of the ten tribes 1 Kgs 12:20
- Led first division of Israel in their journeys Num 10:14
- Commissioned of God to lead in the conquest of the promised land Judg 1:1-3; 4-21
- Made David king 2 Sam 2:1-11; 5:4,5

Zebulun

- "Zebulun shall dwell at the haven of the sea; and he *shall be* for an haven of ships; and his border *shall be* unto Zidon." Gen 49:13
- In Galilee, to the north of Issachar and south of Asher and Naphtali, between the Sea of Galilee and the Mediterranean. Jos 19:10-16
  - According to ancient prophecy this part of Galilee to enjoy a large share of our Lord's public ministry Isa 9:1,2 Mt 4:12-16

Issachar

- Jacob's 9th son, by Leah
  - *sekhari*, "my hire" — Gen 30:18
- The prophetic blessing pronounced by Jacob corresponds with that of Moses — Gen 49:14,15; Deut 33:18,19
- Only Judah and Dan stronger;
  - 64,300 — Num 26:25
  - to 87,000 — 1 Chr 7:5
- Richest portion: Jezreel Valley — 1Chr 12:40

Dan

- "Dan shall be a serpent by the way, an adder in the path, that biteth the horse heels, so that his rider shall fall backward." — Gen 49:7
- First to fall into idolatry — Judg 18:30
- Slighted in genealogies:
  - Names of his sons omitted — Gen 46:23; Num 26:42
  - Name blotted out: — 1 Chr 1-10; Rev 7
  - Mentioned last: — Num 10:25; Jos 19:47-49; 1 Chr 27:16-22

Gad

- Jacob's 7th son, by Zilpah, Leah's handmaid
  - The brother of Asher — Ge 30:11-13; 46:16,18
  - "fortune; luck"
- This tribe was fierce and warlike;
  - they were "strong men of might, men of war for the battle, that could handle shield and buckler, their faces the faces of lions, and like roes upon the mountains for swiftness" — 1Ch 12:8 5:19-22
  - Elijah was of this tribe — 1Ki 17:1

Asher

- "Out of Asher his bread *shall be* fat, and he shall yield royal dainties." Gen 49: 20
  - Settled in northern part: Mt. Lebanon to Med. Incl. Josh 19:24-31
- "Royal Dainties" workmen and materials
  - to David; 2 Sam 5:11
  - ...and Solomon; 1 Kgs 5:1-10
- Kept Passover under Hezekiah (in contrast to others) 2 Chr 30:1,10,11
- To this tribe belonged the prophetess Anna Lk 2:36

Naphtali

- The 5th son of Jacob, the 2nd born to him by Rachel's handmaid, Bilhah. He was full brother of Dan Gen 30:7
  - At his birth Rachel is said to have exclaimed, "wrestlings of God"--i.e. "mighty wrestlings"--"have I wrestled."
- "Naphtali is a hind let loose: he giveth goodly words" Ge 49:21
- N & NW of Sea of Galilee:
  - Capernaum, Bethsaida, Chorazin...

Joseph

- Name means "may he (God) add sons)" Gen 30:24
- Firstborn of Rachel, Jacob's loved wife Gen 30:22-24
- Favored, despised, sold, exalted Gen 37-50
- Over 100 ways a "type" of Christ

Benjamin

- The youngest son of Jacob, called "son of the right hand" by his father
- "Benjamin is a ravenous wolf" Gen 49:27
- Known as ferocious: Judg 19:16; 2 Sam 2:15,16; 1 Chr 8:40; 12:2; 2 Chr 17:17
- Notable heroes include:
  - Ehud, who delivered Israel from the Moabites
  - Saul, the first king (& Jonathan) 1 Sam 9:1
  - Queen Esther Esther 2:5
  - Apostle Paul Rom 11:1

Revelation 7

Judah	Praise the Lord,
Reuben	He has looked on my affliction (and)
Gad	granted good fortune.
Asher	Happy am I,
Napthali	my wrestling
Manasseh	has made me forget my sorrow.
Simeon	God hears me;
Levi	has joined me,
Issachar	purchased me, (and)
Zebulun	exalted me (by)
Joseph	adding to me
Benjamin	the Son of His right hand.

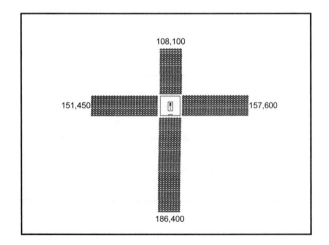

108,100
151,450
157,600
186,400

Genesis Session 24: The Tribes Prophetically

Chapter 49

1) List the sons of Jacob chronologically, with mother, and significance of their name.

2) What *three* forfeitures did Reuben lose, and to whom?

3) List each of the tribes, and their distinctives, and how prophecies were fulfilled in them.

4) When did the "Sceptre depart," and "Shiloh come"?

5) What *two* tribes are not mentioned by name in Revelation 7 and why?

6) Between what two "shoulders" did Benjamin dwell?

Group Discussion Questions: See *Small Group Leaders* section of this workbook.

Congratulations! You're done!

Discussion Questions for Small Group Leaders

Session 1—Introduction and Genesis 1:1

1) How does your world view affect your everyday life? Can you adduce the real world view from one's behavior?

2) Discuss how the Book of Genesis refutes each of the major false philosophies prevalent today.

3) How old do you believe the universe is? *Why* do you believe that? Is the age of the earth any different?

4) What two concepts in mathematics are *not* present in our physical universe? What does that imply about our reality?

5) What does the apparent presence of π and e in the Biblical text signify?

Session 2—Genesis 1:2-5

1) Discuss the possibilities (and problems) with the conjectures of a "gap" between Genesis 1:1 and 1:2.

2) When were the angels created? When did Satan fall?

3) How do changes in the velocity of light impact our world views?

4) Are there exceptions to the entropy laws?

Session 3—Genesis 1:6-8

1) In what way does the Bible anticipate our current discoveries regarding the nature of hyperspaces?

2) Why do some scientists suspect that the entire universe, as we know it, is some kind of synthetic simulation; a subset of an ultimate reality?

3) Why are classical scientists shocked at the findings of quantum physics? How do they impact our own perspectives?

Session 4—Genesis 1:9-13

1) What is the significance of a 3-out-of-4, error-correcting, self-replicating *digital* code in our DNA molecule?

2) Give examples of "irreducible complexity" and the implications for plausible inferences.

3) Defend the concept that our universe is essentially "empty."

4) How do recent discoveries in microbiology refute evolution?

5) How does the process of photosynthesis refute evolution?

6) How does the current approaches to the "Search for Extraterrestrial Intelligence" (SETI) contradict the premises of evolutionary thought?

Session 5—Genesis 1:14-19

1) What are the two major views of cosmology and which do you favor?

2) What do the signs of the Mazzeroth (Zodiac) imply concerning the history of man's view of the heavens?

3) Is it possible that the creation of the earth preceded the rest of the universe?

Session 6—Genesis 1:20-23

1) List the major problems with "evolution" (biogenesis) as an explanation of our origin.

2) Discuss personal examples in which careful *coordination* is required among members of a design group. How does this impact the potential role of randomness as a process?

3) How does the complexity of even the "simplest" living cell refute the notion of it having occurred by random unaided processes?

4) How does the process of photosynthesis refute the theory of evolution?

5) How does your views regarding evolution impact your reading of the Bible?

Session 7—Genesis 1:24-28

1) What do Fibonacci numbers reveal about our Creator?

2) What are the main features of the human anatomy that refute accidental, unaided chance as an explanation for our origin?

Session 8—Genesis 2

1) Discuss the role of the Sabbath in the New Testament. What are the implications for Christians today?

2) Are the practices of the early church a *reliable* guide for us today? Why or why not?

Session 9—Genesis 3

1) In what ways is the marriage union a theological model of eternal truths?

2) Discuss examples where "God always does the seeking": in the Bible *and* in your personal life.

3) When did Israel begin? How does this affect the geopolitical and sociological horizons today?

4) Give examples of "fig leaves" of man's religious efforts today.

5) Why does God allow Satan to continue?

Session 10—Genesis 4-5

1) How were the spiritual attitudes of Cain and Abel different?

2) What inferences can be drawn from the genealogy in Genesis 5?

3) What inferences can be drawn from the genealogy of Cain's descendants in Genesis 4?

4) Compare and contrast the two trees: in the Garden of Eden and the Cross at Golgatha.

Session 11—Genesis 6

1) Compare and contrast the "Angel view" and "lines of Seth" view of Genesis 6. Which do you favor?

2) Where is *Tartarus*? How do *Hades*, *Sheol*, and *Gehenna* differ?

3) Discuss the similarities (and contrasts) of Genesis 6 with Greek mythology.

4) Who were the *Rephaim* in the Old Testament? Where did they come from?

5) Discuss events, and the participants, in the dialogs recorded in Psalm 2.

Session 12—Genesis 7-8

1) How big was the ark (in modern terms)? How many species could it have contained? How many were there to be contained?

2) Discuss the strengths and weaknesses of two prevailing views: a) Water canopy theory; b) Hydroplate theory. What do you think happened?

3) What three groups of people faced the flood and how were they distinctly dealt with? What are the eschatological inferences therein?

4) Is the Ark on Mt. Ararat in Turkey, or is it in Iran?

Session 13—Genesis 9-10

1) Is capital punishment appropriate today?

2) Is it Biblically appropriate to eat meat?

3) Should grape juice be substituted during Communion?

4) Where is the United States represented in Bible prophecy?

Session 14—Genesis 11

1) Discuss the perspective that the entire Bible is a "tale of two cities": Babylon and Jerusalem.

2) What is the significance of the rebuilt Babylon in Iraq today?

3) Is there a relationship between the Vatican and the Woman of Revelation 17?

Session 15—Genesis 12-15

1) How is Genesis 12:2,3 relevant to our world today? To the U.S. in particular?

2) Should Christians go to war?

3) Who was Melchizedek and why is he significant?

4) How is the Abrahamic Covenant relevant to the tensions in the Middle East today?

Session 16—Genesis 16-20

1) In what ways did Ishmael and Isaac reflect the analogy between the "flesh" and the "spirit"?

2) Give examples of a "circumcised" heart.

3) What are the *prophetic* implications of the parable of the woman and the leaven in Matthew 13:33? How does this relate to the passage in Gen 18?

4) Discuss the implications if only *one* "righteous" was left in Sodom. What does this imply *prophetically?*

5) If Jesus could have spared Capernaum (Mt 11:23), why didn't He?

Session 17—Genesis 21, 22, and 24

1) Explain the contrasting analogy that Paul makes between the "bondwoman" and the "freewoman." How do we apply this to our own lives?

2) What other examples of "types" do we find in the Bible? What are the "dangers" of using "types" for *doctrine*?

3) What other examples of "Gentile" marriages are there in the Bible and what might they signify?

4) Compare Ruth 3 and 4 to Genesis 24.

Session 18—Genesis 23, 25-27

1) What is an "Arab"?

2) What are the dangers of parental favoritism in the family? Of spiritual insensitivity? Of deceptions?

3) Did God accomplish His will through the deceptions within the family or despite them? Were they necessary or were they distractions?

4) Discuss the alternative approaches to studying the Word of God and their respective strengths and weakenesses.

Session 19—Genesis 28-31

1) Explain who the *Rephaim* were. Why were they a danger to God's plan?

2) Are there *teraphims* in our lives?

3) Review the ways that the Land Covenant to Israel is being challenged in today's current events.

4) Review the ancient tribal hatreds and why there will not be any real peace in the Middle East until the Prince of Peace comes.

Session 20—Genesis 32-36

1) What was the real significance of the all-night wrestling match?

2) Are there "strange gods" co-existing in our lives? What are we to do with them?

Session 21—Genesis 37-39

1) Discuss the many ways that the Book of Ruth is a foreshadowing of God's program for the *church*.

2) Why do we suspect that Potiphar didn't really believe his wife?

Session 22—Genesis 40-45

1) What may be the significance of *two* in a) the number of dreams in his childhood; b) the number imprisonments; c) the number of dreamers in prison; d) the number of Pharaoh's dreams?

2) Was it appropriate for Joseph to *charge* for the dispensation of food to the hungry?

3) Why do we suspect that Jacob had his suspicions about the fate of Joseph?

4) Discuss the manner in which Joseph handled his brothers on their 1st and 2nd visits to Egypt. Why did he do what he did, and what was accomplished?

Session 23—Genesis 46-48, 50

1) Review Joseph's stewardship for Pharaoh and the impact on subsequent Egyptian history.

2) Contrast the bypassing of the firstborn for four generations.

Session 24—Genesis 49

1) What were the main lessons *you* learned in this tour through Genesis?

2) How has it impacted your life?

3) What is the most compelling reason you regard the Bible is true?

4) What is the most compelling reason to take Jesus Christ seriously?

5) *How* do you "take Jesus Christ seriously"?

Koinonia Institute

Book of Genesis I (BIB 201) 3 credits
Sessions 1-14

Book of Genesis II (BIB 202) 3 credits
Sessions 15-24

Property of:

Name_____ Date_____

Address_____

City_____ State_____ Zip_____

Workbook Grade_____ Assignment Grade_____

Copyright © 2004, Koinonia Institute. All rights reserved. This publication may not be reproduced in part by any means without permission from Koinonia Institute, Coeur d'Alene, Idaho.

Instructions

For maximum benefit, the student should proceed as follows:

1. Before completing assignments the student should familiarize him/herself with the entire workbook. BIB 201 covers sessions 1-14; BIB 202, sessions 15-24.

2. As unfamiliar words are discovered, they should be listed, looked up in the dictionary, and definitions should be written in the provided space (Glossary of New Terms) for reference. Feel free to add more pages if necessary.

3. All writing assignments must follow the procedures described in *Guidelines for Writing Assignments,* including format and title page.

4. Send completed work (including this workbook and all assignments) at the end of each course to Koinonia Institute for grading. Your graded materials will be returned to you as soon as possible with a sealed envelope containing your final exam(s).

5. Carefully review the materials, all assignments, and your study notes in preparation for your final exam(s).

6. Final exams should remain sealed until all review work is complete. Your study materials, workbook, notes, and assignments must be put away, and you must have an observer to witness the integrity of the final exam. The observer must sign the exam title page at the designated place.

7. Please note that you will receive a separate grade for study questions—both existing ones and the ones you create (25%); research assignments (25%); and, the final exam (50%). These grades will be averaged to determine the final course grade. There is no grade given for the session handouts—use them as you wish to help you complete the study questions and/or assignments.

8. Remember to place your name on everything you send in and retain a copy for your protection.

GRADING SCALE
A = 93-100
B = 85-92
C = 76-84
D = 70-75
F   Below 70

Glossary of New Terms

Multiple-Choice Questions

Assignment: Create ten (10) multiple choice questions for each session (1-14 for BIB 201/15-24 for BIB 202). Be sure to cover the breadth of the entire session. Questions will be graded on content, insight and difficulty. Accompany questions/answers with Scriptural/ resource reference. Use the format example below and be sure to circle the correct answer.

1. _____

    A. _____

    B. _____

    C. _____

    D. _____

Essay Questions

Assignment: Create three (3) essay questions for each session (1-14 for BIB 201/15-24 for BIB 202). Be sure to cover the breadth of the entire session. Questions will be graded on content, insight and difficulty. Accompany questions/answers with Scriptural/resource reference. Use format below as an example.

Question 1. _____

_____
_____
_____
_____
_____

Answer _____

_____
_____
_____
_____
_____
_____
_____
_____
_____
_____
_____
_____
_____
_____

Candidate Research Projects

Assignment: Choose five (5) from the list of candidate research projects for each course (sessions 1-14 for BIB 201/15-24 for BIB 202). Follow the procedures found in the *Guidelines for Writing Assignments* for Compositions. You may choose up to 2 "list" assignments per course; the other three should be compositions (3 or more pages in length).

Session 1:
1) Compile a list of Genesis references in the New Testament.
2) Compile a list of physical factors that indicate a young earth. (Walt Brown lists 100.)
3) Compile a list of problems with the various alternative views of the "Big Bang."

Session 2:
1) Compile the arguments for (and against) a "gap" between Genesis 1:1 and 1:2.
2) Contrast the characteristics of angels, fallen angels, and demons as presented in the Bible.
3) Compile a history of the views concerning the nature of light from earliest times to the present day.
4) Compile a summary of widely held scientific views that ultimately were proven incorrect.

Session 3:
1) List the primary versions of "Big Bang" models and discuss their fatal shortcomings.
2) Explore the various paradoxes emerging from quantum physics and their implications in understanding our universe.
3) Explore the role of hyperspaces in our contemporary perspectives.

Session 4:
1) Compile a catalog of examples of the anthropic principle. Explore the implications of variability in each.
2) Compile a list of examples where scientific discoveries were *anticipated* in the Scriptures.
3) Compile background on the missing (95%!) "dark matter" in the universe and the major theories and conjectures supporting the searches.

Session 5:
1) In what ways is the Book of Joshua an anticipatory model of the Book of Revelation? List and detail.
2) Compile a list of scientific enigmas emerging from the Book of Job.
3) In what ways does the *Mazzeroth* seem to portray God's plan of redemption? Compile a detailed profile with supporting sources.

Session 6:
1) Analyze a complex creature in terms of its design problems and the likelihood of it having occurred by unaided random chance.

Session 7:
1) Compile a list of references to the Trinity in the Old Testament.
2) Compile a list of design interdependencies of the major systems of the human body.
3) Compile a list of occurrences of Fibonacci numbers in nature, our society, art, or other areas of discovery.
4) Build a detailed model of the Temple of Solomon.

Session 8:
1) What is the evidence for Sunday replacing Saturday as the "Sabbath?"
2) Compile a list of the principal edicts and their significance during the Fourth Century.

Session 9:
1) Compile examples where the marriage union is used in the Bible to convey theological or prophetic insights.
2) Trace the apparent linkages of serpents in history and literature with evil, Satan, etc.
3) Compile examples of scientific discoveries that are consistent with Genesis 3.

Session 10:
1) Trace the role of blood sacrifices from Genesis 3:21 to Crucifixion of Christ.

Session 11:
1) Trace the evidences of giants throughout history.
2) Trace the legends of "star people," demigods, and the like in ancient mythologies.
3) Trace the additional references which impact our understanding of the dialogs in Psalm 2.

Session 12:
1) Research the records and publications supporting the location of the ark on Mt. Ararat in Turkey and contrast them with the possibilities that it may yet lie in the region *east* of Babylon.
2) Contrast in detail the canopy theory (re: Henry Morris) and the hydroplate theories (Walt Brown) of the flood. [Don Patten believes the planet Mars may also have been involved.]

Session 13:
1) Develop a map of the regional nationalities summarized in Genesis 10. While many remain problematical, highlight the most significant ones. Highlight the prophetically relevant ones.
2) Explore the role (and risks) of wine as portrayed in the Bible. [Is a grape juice substitute really Biblical?]

Session 14:
1) Review the possible relationship between the Vatican and the Woman of Revelation 17. [Cf. Dave Hunt, *A Woman Rides the Beast.*]
2) Explore the view that the 12 tribes are represented in the Hebrew *Mazzeroth*, and profile the God's plan of redemption.

Session 15:
1) Compile the Biblical basis for Israel's right to the land that is being challenged today. [*Betrayal of the Chosen*, Koinonia House.]
2) Investigate the legitimacy of the plight of the Palestinians in the land of Israel today. [Joan Peters, *From Time Immemorial,* McMillan & Co.]

Session 16:
1) Compare the seven kingdom parables (Mt 13) with the Letters to the Seven Churches (Rev 2 & 3).
2) Compile a list of commonly held superstitions and scientific errors that are *not* found in the Bible.
3) Compile a list of scientific discoveries that are *anticipated* in the Bible.

Session 17:
1) Make a list of illustrative "types" in the Bible and their significance.
2) List the prophetic specifications that were fulfilled in the Crucifixion of Christ.
3) List the details that would seem to indicate that the "Garden Tomb" in Jerusalem is, indeed, the actual tomb from which Christ was resurrected.

Session 18:
1) What is an "Arab"? How does confusion on this issue complicate our understanding of current events in the Middle East?
2) Study the role of Edom and its associated region in end time prophecy.

Session 19:
1) Trace the listings of the Tribes of Israel in the Bible and their distinctives.

Session 20:
1) Review the destiny of Petra ("Bozrah" in Edom) in the end times. (Cf. The Briefing Pack, *The Next Holocaust and the Refuge in Edom*.)

Session 21:
1) Compile a list of the utilization of dreams in the Bible. (What do you conclude?)
2) List the reasons that the "woman" of Revelation 12 is Israel and not the church.
3) Research the several ways that "levirate marriages" are involved in the genealogy of Jesus Christ.
4) Begin a list of ways that Joseph can be viewed as a "type" of Jesus Christ. (Continue in the subsequent chapters…)

Session 22:
1) Trace the use of bread and wine throughout the entire Bible.
2) Trace the use of "three days" throughout the Scripture.
3) Trace the use of birds as adversatives in the Scripture.
4) Continue compiling your list of possible parallels between Joseph and Jesus Christ.

Session 23:
1) Complete your list of the ways that the narrative of Joseph can be viewed as a prefiguring of Jesus Christ. (A.W. Pink lists over 100, but that may be stretching things a bit!)

Session 24:
1) Make a detailed study of the *Mazzeroth* as a portrayal of God's plan of redemption.
2) Construct a model of the Camp of Israel, with the Tabernacle and its furnishings, etc.
3) Explore the ostensible validity (or rebuttals) to the notion of the "Ten Lost Tribes." Where does this concept come from? Is it Biblically sound?

REVIEW

IN PREPARATION FOR THE FINAL EXAM FOR THE COURSE(S), REVIEW ALL ACTIVITIES IN THE STUDY GUIDE. REFER TO THE COURSE MATERIALS ON ISSUES THAT HAVE BEEN MORE CHALLENGING. ONCE YOU ARE CONFIDENT OF MASTERY OF THE SUBJECT THEN PROCEED TO THE FINAL TEST. TEST QUESTIONS WILL COVER THE SCOPE OF THIS COURSE (SESSIONS 1-14 FOR BIB 201/SESSIONS 15-24 FOR BIB 202).